T AYLESBURY

Continued on the back endpaper

THOMAS HICKMAN CHARITY

1698 ~ 1998

Thomas Hickman's Charity, Aylesbury

A Tercentenary History
1698–1998

"As long as this world continueth. …"

HUGH HANLEY

2000

First published in 2000 by
LEOPARD'S HEAD PRESS LIMITED
1–5 Broad Street, Oxford, OX1 3AW

ISBN 0 904920 39 9

Typeset by Cambrian Typesetters
Frimley, Surrey
Printed in Great Britain

Contents

Acknowledgements

I wish to thank Graham Aylett, Chairman of the Thomas Hickman Trustees, for his unfailing support and for practical assistance which included reading and commenting on successive drafts of this history and help with selecting and captioning the illustrations. I am grateful, too, to Roger Bettridge for kindly reading an earlier version of the main text and suggesting improvements. Others who helped in various ways included: Susanne Spinks of Parrott and Coales, who saw to it that I had instant access to relevant documents in the firm's custody; Ian Toplis who briefed me on William White, the architect; Ray Shrimpton and Lesley Williams of the Buckinghamshire Family History Society who supplied printouts from databases in their care; and the staffs of the County Record Office and the Local Studies Library whose courtesy and professionalism greatly eased my path.

The Trustees wish to thank the following for permission to reproduce illustrations (for serial numbers in round brackets see list of illustrations): Aylesbury Town Centre Partnership (plates 1, 3, 4, 5; all copyright Kevin Sansbury Photography); Rachel Beckett (frontispiece; 31); British Library Newspaper Library (22); Buckinghamshire Record Office (2, 5, 6, 12, 16, 27, 35; cover illustration); Buckinghamshire Local Studies Library (18); *The Bucks Herald* (plates 2, 7; 3, 36, 39); James Cox Associates (32, 37, 38, 40, 41); Sergio Cruz (endpapers); Bernard Hall (1, 4, 13, 15, 23, 25, 30, 33, 34); Ordnance Survey (41); Victoria and Albert Museum (10, 11, 14, 17); John Vince (28).

Foreword

Thomas Hickman, founder of the Charity, was clear about the value of continuity. Writing in 1695, planning the creation of his Foundation, he looked ahead to the beneficiaries drawing comfort from it "as long as this world continueth".

At the start of a new Millennium, his present Trustees remain especially mindful of his bidding to look well ahead, building on what has been achieved in the last 300 years so that our successors may continue for the foreseeable future to afford help to the Aylesburians whose needs are greatest.

The seeds of the idea for this book about **Thomas Hickman**, which also looks back over the first three centuries of his Foundation's work, were sown by some of the present Hickman Residents. When they asked who **Thomas Hickman** was, and how he came to set up his Charity, the Trustees found they had only the vaguest idea, and nobody else knew more.

Therefore when, after the service of thanksgiving in St. Mary's Church on 11 June 1998, the Residents and many others associated with Hickman's gathered in the Museum garden for a great party to celebrate the three hundredth birthday of the Foundation, the Trustees promised that they would let everyone know whatever could be found out about our Founder. They were delighted to be able to commission Hugh Hanley, former Buckinghamshire County Archivist and a great authority on the history of Aylesbury, to undertake the research.

You have the results in your hands. As you may perceive, it has proved a far from easy job, and the Trustees are deeply grateful to Hugh Hanley for the care, insight and time he has devoted to the work. If his book should also serve as a means of bringing to light any additional material connected with **Thomas Hickman**, the Trustees would be very grateful to learn of it.

Meanwhile, the essential work of the Trust continues. While this remains best known through the provision of residences in central Aylesbury on the site of the original 1698 almshouses and the adjacent area, simply to provide housing is by no means enough, especially nowadays.

Our intention is to continue into the new Millennium not only all those responsibilities in respect of those whom our Trust's Scheme quaintly refers to as "almspersons" – the Hickman Residents – but also to work more and more closely with other organisations with expertise or other resources relevant to Aylesbury people. This we can do within the terms of our Scheme which relate to relief in need.

We have long worked closely with our sister Charity, William Harding's; greatly assisted by Parrott & Coales who act as Clerks to the Trustees of both bodies. More recently we have extended and tested this co-operation, working with the Citizens Advice Bureau and Age Concern for example. Our aim is to facilitate their help for individual Aylesbury residents, working in partnership where appropriate, whilst not taking on their responsibilities. This is proving successful; we plan to extend our work in this way.

In particular, we are seeking to secure coherent, consistent help for residents of Aylesbury in greatest need, hardship or distress. So far, we have identified three main ways in which **Thomas Hickman's Charity** can do this:

- try to minimise any gaps between the respective roles of other bodies which help Aylesbury people demonstrably in need;
- act swiftly, flexibly and directly where necessary to prevent further harm to those within the objectives of the Charity; and
- identify any long-term means by which to lessen or prevent distress to Aylesbury people in future and follow it.

Of course, in the last hundred or so years, local authorities and other bodies which draw on public funds have been set up to work in the field of social need (and we do not apply any of the Charity's funds directly in relief of rates, taxes or other public funds). Our Foundation has already been working about three times as long and our endeavour (and, we trust, that of our successors) is to continue and extend its role as described above in line with the vision and foresight of **Thomas Hickman**, throughout the next 300 years: and, we pray, "as long as this world continueth". Meanwhile, we hope you will enjoy this account of what has gone before …

January 2000   *Chairman, Thomas Hickman's Trustees*
10 St Mary's Square, Aylesbury

List of Illustrations

Colour Illustrations

Frontispiece.
Design by Rachel Beckett to commemorate the tercentenary of Thomas Hickman's Charity in 1998.

Between pages 46 and 47
Plate 1   The original almshouses seen through the churchyard gate.
Plate 2   Wall plaque on No. 8 Church Street.
Plate 3   The original almshouses, showing frontage to Parsons Fee.
Plate 4   Adjoining houses in Church Street more recently acquired.
Plate 5   St Mary's parish church, seen from Church Street.
Plate 6   No. 8 (The Chantry) and No. 10 Church Street.
Plate 7   Secret Gardens. Residents' bric-a-brac stall in the Chantry gardens.
Plate 8   At home in one of the Charity's converted houses in Castle Street.

Black and White Illustrations

Endpapers
Church Street, Aylesbury. From a drawing by Sergio Cruz.

Cover Illustration
Architectural drawings for rebuilding the almshouses, by William White, 1865, showing elevations.

List of Figures

1

The Foundation

THOMAS HICKMAN'S Charity owes its existence to the will of Thomas Hickman of Aylesbury, gentleman, the registered copy of which is dated 1 January 1696 (1695 Old Style) with the addition of a short deathbed codicil dated 19 April 1698, only three days before the entry in the parish register announcing the burial of "Mr Thomas Hickman" on 22 April.[1] By his will, further details of which are discussed in chapter 3, Thomas left all his property consisting of the "messuage," or house, in Temple Street "in which I now dwell" (now No. 1 Church Street, but formerly known only as *Hickman's*), five cottages, four of them occupied, near the church gate (later Nos. 1–4 Parsons Fee and No. 16 Church Street), a house in the market place adjoining the passage to the King's Head on the east (now No. 11 Market Square), and a cottage, farmhouse and some 32 acres of land in the hamlet of Walton, to be held in trust and "never to be sold." The three trustees named in the will were the testator's "kinsmen" Robert Hickman of Aylesbury, carpenter, Joseph Claydon of Bishopstone, in the parish of Stone, yeoman, and John Plater of Haddenham, yeoman, who were each to have £1 a year for their trouble. They were to apply the rents and profits of the property in the first instance to raise and pay in succession five pecuniary legacies of £100 apiece for the benefit of several of the testator's relations. When this had been done, and only then, the trustees, together with the churchwardens and overseers of the poor of Aylesbury, were to apply the annual income:

> to the poorest people and most pitifull objects of Charity in Alms to them, and not to ease the rich[2] in their Collection [i.e. the parish poor rate] but

1 Buckinghamshire Record Office (BRO) D/A/We/45/169. See abstract in Appendix 2. A fairly detailed abstract is printed in G. Lipscomb, *History and Antiquities of the County of Buckingham* (1847), vol. 2, pp. 50–51. The original will does not survive.

2 Erroneously transcribed as "parish" in *Reports of the Commissioners for Inquiring Concerning Charities, 26th Report* (1833), pp. 50–53.

this my gift is given that they may have a more comfortable subsistence in their poor and mean Condition as long as this world continueth.

Additionally, once the legacies had been discharged, the five cottages were to become almshouses for poor people of the town to dwell in, at the direction of the churchwardens and overseers and the trustees. There was, however, one important proviso, which was that:

> if any of my kindred though never so farr of[f] or living in the towne will accept of any one of the appartments as they now are and will live there and their Children after them shall at any time or times hereafter take their Choice of any of the said appartments, whether they be poor or rich[3] for their lives and I do give them full power and Authority to enter therein and dwell as aforesaid And I do order my said Trustees and the said officers to assist them therein they keeping them in tenantable repairs, lett them be one two three or more of my kindred So I would not lett them want an habitation Seeing I have given so largely to the said towne ...

The will went on to list some further miscellaneous bequests. The testator's cousin Faith Plater, "who now lives with me," was to receive £50; the poor of Aylesbury were to have £15; and £30 was allocated to funeral expenses, all to be paid out of sums which the testator was owed by five separate individuals upon security. In addition the poor of Wendover and Great Brickhill were to receive gifts of £1 10s. to each parish; the reasons for these gifts are not stated, but they must surely reflect personal links of some kind – whether direct or indirect – with both places.

There followed some more small pecuniary legacies to various other cousins and, finally, the residue of the testator's "chattels, money, plate, rings and other things" was assigned to Robert Hickman and Faith Plater, who were named joint executors. The testator's "loving friend" Doctor John Wilson of Hartwell was named as overseer of the will and was to have 20 shillings for his pains. This was the only such payment to a non-relation.

The codicil, which Thomas – now almost too weak to hold a pen – attested with an illiterate's mark, was concerned chiefly with the disposal of additional landed property which the testator had lately purchased from one Thomas Hoare, the location and extent of which were not stated. This property too was devised to the trustees with instructions to sell as much of it as was necessary to satisfy all the testator's debts and legacies and to retain the rest on the same terms and

---

3 Transcribed as "sick", *ibid.*

Back view of the original almshouses in Parsons Fee, with St Mary's church beyond, showing part of the former garden of No. 12 Church Street.

conditions as the property devised in the will. The effect of this – assuming that the newly-acquired property was worth at least £500 – was to free the estate of obligations which would otherwise have taken many years to pay off at the current rates of rent (which would probably not have brought in much more than £30 per annum) so that the charity now took immediate effect. The likelihood is that the purchase was financed out of the residuary personal estate left to Robert Hickman and Faith Plater. If so, the decision to transfer assets in this way could be connected to Faith's marriage some six months previously.

In his codicil Thomas also remembered his servant Katherine Plater (she was also his cousin) who was given one of the five cottages for her lifetime. She thus became the first of many relations of the founder to be accorded this privilege, though it is not known whether in fact she availed herself of it.

The will was proved on 24 July 1699, over a year after Thomas's death. The delay was an unusually long one. It must have been due – at least in part – to the arrangements needed to comply with the instructions in the codicil regarding the sale of the most recently acquired land.

Housing the Aylesbury Poor

Almshouses were not new to Aylesbury. Prior to the Reformation the Fraternity of the Blessed Virgin Mary, whose "Brotherhood House" was in Church Street, was supporting ten almshouses and four cottages in which poor people lived rent free[4]. Earlier still, the twelfth-century hospitals of St Leonard and St John the Baptist probably more resembled almshouses than modern hospitals. Nor did almshouses entirely disappear with the old religion. According to a record made in 1688 the churchwardens and overseers of the poor were then responsible for no fewer than sixteen or seventeen almshouses, variously acquired, all located in the immediate vicinity of the churchyard and in Green End, which provided accommodation for twenty or more poor people.[5] Some of these had been built at parish expense; others had been given or devised over the years by benefactors such as William Cockman, who is said to have given the parish four almshouses in 1589. Two of the almshouses at Green End antedated the Reformation, being the gift of Thomas Elliott in 1494.[6]

These parish almshouses – "poorhouses" might be a more accurate description

---

4 John Chenevix Trench and Pauline Fenley, "The County Museum Buildings, Church Street, Aylesbury", in *Records of Buckinghamshire*, vol. 33 (1993, for 1991), p. 15.

5 Robert Gibbs, *History of Aylesbury* (1885), pp. 390–391; BRO PR 11/5/1, copy memorandum at front of volume of churchwardens' accounts for 1749–87.

6 Gibbs, pp. 465, 471.

– were not separately administered at this period, but were treated by the authorities as just one of several resources for dealing with the problems of poverty and homelessness, problems which were rapidly increasing in Aylesbury in the closing decades of the seventeenth century, fuelled by inward migration from the countryside. Another expedient favoured at this time, and one from which Thomas Hickman had himself benefited in his capacity of landlord, was for the parish to pay the rents of poor parishioners. Later, in 1702, this policy of paying rents from the poor rate was abandoned in the interests of economy and

The badge of poverty. In 1697 those in receipt of poor relief from the parish authorities were subjected to harsh new legislation which required them to wear distinctive badges. No example from Aylesbury is known but this one from Wooburn parish shows what such paupers' badges looked like (Brass – size 56 mm × 77 mm)

instead the almshouses were enlarged to provide additional accommodation for the poor. Meanwhile, in 1697, the parish overseers were beginning to enforce harsh new legislation which required those in receipt of poor relief to wear badges.[7]

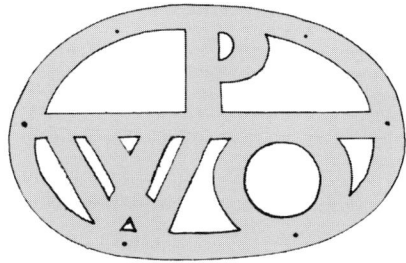

Aylesbury's First Endowed Almshouses

It is against this background that Thomas Hickman's Charity, Aylesbury's first and only independent, privately-endowed charity, was founded. But it needs also to be seen in the context of other new, privately-endowed, foundations elsewhere, of which there were a good many in the seventeenth century. Local examples include the Weedon almshouses at Chesham, founded by a local draper in 1624; the Drake almshouses at Amersham, founded by the lord of the manor in 1657; and the Winwood almshouses at Quainton, another gentry foundation of 1685.[8] What these had in common was that they all conformed to the conventional pattern, doubtless derived from medieval tradition, of purpose-built, single-occupancy units designated from the first for a stated number of poor people who were invariably provided with a weekly stipend or pension.

Thomas Hickman's almshouses were different. In the first place the houses

---

7 *Victoria History of the Counties of England: Buckinghamshire* (*VCH*), vol. 2 (1908), p. 80; W. Le Hardy and G. L. Reckitt (eds.), *Buckinghamshire Sessions Records*, vol. 2 (Aylesbury 1936), p. 144.
8 *VCH*, vol. 3 (1925), pp. 141–2, 217, vol. 4 (1927), pp. 92, 99.

were not new, nor – at that time – did they differ significantly in appearance or size from the other houses round about them. As a result, although the three houses which were wholly situated in Parsons Fee were smaller than the others, they were all large compared to conventional almshouses and were so described by the Commissioners for Inquiring into Charities in the 1830s. They were different, too, in having no prescribed limit on the number of occupants and in making no provision for the maintenance of the occupants, so that, unless they possessed other means of support, they would be dependent on the poor rate for subsistence. But what was particularly unusual about Hickman's foundation was the privilege it extended to the founder's kin.

The principle that the relations of the founder of a charitable institution should enjoy some form of privileged access, though it appears to be the exception in local charities, was not uncommon in public schools and university colleges. Generations of the Bell family of Aylesbury, for example, benefited educationally from their claim, proudly recorded on one of the family monuments, to be founder's kin of New College, Oxford.[9] What was exceptional – even eccentric – about Hickman's was the open-ended, unconditional commitment that any kin, whether poor or not, should be allowed priority of access to the almshouses. This clause can be seen as essentially at variance with the idea of a public charity and as giving the foundation something of the character of a family trust. Hickman obviously thought that he had struck a balance between public and private ("Seeing I have given so largely to the said towne"), but is there a hint of defensiveness in his tone?

In addition there were some obvious weaknesses in the other arrangements laid down in the will. The annual distribution money for the poor of Aylesbury was not "ring-fenced," but was in effect to be the residue of the income from the endowment and so could easily be swallowed up in expenses or even diverted to provide a dole for kin who happened to be in need. The three original trustees were themselves kin and thus had a vested interest in the charity's resources and in how they were deployed. Moreover, no formal mechanism for ensuring the continuity of succession to the trusteeship was prescribed, nor was any definition of acceptable kinship given. In the circumstances difficulties were almost bound to arise, and, as will be seen, so it proved for almost the first two centuries of the charity's existence.

---

9 Gibbs, *Aylesbury*, p. 39; Joseph Foster, *Alumni Oxonienses 1500–1714* (1890–91, reprinted 1968).

2

The Founder: Thomas Hickman
(1637?–1698)

Who was Thomas Hickman? Despite the public nature of his benefaction he remains an elusive figure. Most of what is known for certain about him is contained in his will, quoted above, which though by no means uninformative, raises more questions than it answers. In his preamble Thomas directs that his body is to be buried "in the grave of my dear mother digged as deep again as any grave is now adays made," from which, and from the absence of any reference to a wife or children, living or dead, it is probably safe to conclude that he died a bachelor. As we shall see, he appears to have been sixty years old when he died and the will makes clear that he had no close relations living. His situation thus closely resembled those of two other local benefactors, his younger contemporaries William Harding, founder of Harding's Charity, and Henry Phillips, who re-endowed Aylesbury's Free Grammar School in 1714. Where he differed from these was in the degree of family obligation which he paradoxically felt. For in addition to the general clause about his kin already cited, he remembered by name in his will no fewer than nineteen individuals – living and dead – who were more or less remotely related to him, the closest being a solitary deceased uncle, and he left legacies totalling over £500 to them and their children.

However, Thomas was on close personal terms with at least two of his kin. At the time he made his will in January 1696, being then "of good health of body," he was living with his unmarried cousin, Faith Plater, who evidently acted as his housekeeper, and at the time of his death two years later he was, as we have seen, being looked after by another female relation, Faith's sister, Katherine Plater. Faith's association with Thomas Hickman went back several years at least because her signature appears alongside Thomas's as a witness to local wills made in 1691 and 1694.[10]

10 A. W. Attwood, "Abstract of Registered Wills Proved in the Archdeaconry Court of Buckingham 1686–1695"(undated typescript in County Reference Library).

Prized Possessions

Thomas was clearly a man of some cultivation for his most prized personal possessions and the only ones to be specified in his will were his books and his mathematical instruments, which were to go to his cousin Robert Hickman, the carpenter, who was also his trustee and executor, "except some good books that my cozen Faith may like to read."

Mathematical instruments at this date meant instruments for the measurement of distances and angles and for putting them on paper in the form of drawings. They were used by practical people such as surveyors and architects – though these scarcely amounted to full-time professions at the time – and probably by master carpenters engaged on larger projects which required a measure of planning, such as house-building. They could also have been owned by landowners of a practical turn of mind and, more generally, by persons with an interest in the study or teaching of mathematics. Interest in the subject was quite widespread among educated people in this, the age of Isaac Newton and the Royal

Book on Mathematics showing frontispiece inscribed in Latin by Rev. Ralph Gladman (d. 1725), master of Aylesbury Grammar School. Thomas Hickman bequeathed mathematical instruments and books to his kinsman and trustee, Robert Hickman, a carpenter

Society. One of the books in the personal library of Ralph Gladman, master of the grammar school from the late 1680s, which he bequeathed to the school, was a copy of a Latin work on mathematics published in 1668, though its pristine condition suggests that it was not much consulted.[11]

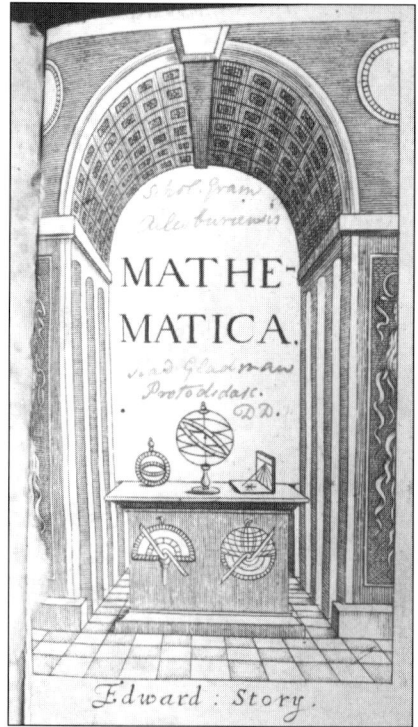

11 I am grateful to Mr John R. Millburn for information on mathematical instruments; Ralph Gladman's book, which was restored to the school in 1998, is described in the *Bucks Herald* of 21 Oct. 1998.

"Hickman's"

As befitted a self-styled gentleman, Thomas resided in one of the quieter residential parts of the town, which was already being favoured by lawyers and other professional men. We must be careful not to exaggerate the appeal of the area at this time: for in 1698 Thomas's new trustees were in trouble for laying a dunghill in the public street, and as late as 1779 it was felt necessary to forbid the presence of pigs in the churchyard; but at least it was removed from the hustle and bustle of the market place.[12] Thomas's house, which still stands and remains in the ownership of the Trust, is described in the will as being enclosed within walls of brick, still a relatively new and fashionable building material in Aylesbury. The building itself had not yet acquired its present elegant brick facade, but was a substantial two-storey timber-framed structure of sixteenth-century date, with a projecting upper storey similar to surviving ancient cottages in Parsons Fee. Most of the original timbers are still intact. The massive moulded ceiling beams in the interior of the ground floor are much as Thomas Hickman would have known them; they point to there having been only two rooms, since subdivided, on this floor. Thomas would also recognise the staircase, part of which, including the great central oak post, is original.[13]

Interior of Thomas Hickman's house (now No. 1 Church Street) in the quieter residential part of Aylesbury. Although re-fronted since his time, many of the interior features like this staircase to the first floor and (right) sixteenth-century oak post remain and would have been familiar to him.

---

12   BRO D/BASM/5A/1, court rolls of Prebendal manor; Gibbs, *Aylesbury,* p. 56.
13   Hayward Parrott, "No. 1 Church Street", in *Aylesbury Town Yesterdays* (1982).

Friends and Acquaintances

The will shows that Thomas numbered among his acquaintances several persons of considerable standing locally. His friend, Dr John Wilson of Hartwell, who was to oversee the performance of his will, is identifiable as the John Wilson, doctor of physic, who died at Aylesbury in 1712 leaving £80 for apprenticing poor children. University-educated physicians could command fees that only the rich could afford and they were still something of a rarity in rural areas in 1696. Dr Wilson's career, as pieced together mainly from the reference books, had been an unorthodox one, but it can be paralleled in the careers of a good many other professional men of his generation. Born probably around 1630, he graduated B.A. from New Inn Hall, Oxford, in 1649 and was appointed master of the free grammar school at Aylesbury in 1655, too late for Thomas Hickman to have been one of his pupils. In 1657 he became rector of Hulcott, where he displaced the existing Royalist rector. At the Restoration, like hundreds of other non-conforming clergy, he was ejected from his living and found refuge as chaplain first to Sir Thomas Lee of Hartwell and later to Lee's stepfather, Sir Richard Ingoldsby of Waldridge in Dinton. Both were former Parliamentarians who had made their peace with Charles II and could be expected to show sympathy to a Puritan ex-rector. Ingoldsby (1617–85), who was cousin to Oliver Cromwell and had actually signed Charles I's death warrant, was fortunate indeed to have escaped the dire fate reserved for the regicides which Aylesbury's former M.P., Thomas Scot, had undergone. The political support which Lee and Ingoldsby enjoyed in Aylesbury was such that they were able to occupy the borough's two seats in Parliament for the whole of Charles II's reign. Wilson later "betook himself to the Practice of Physic," apparently without any formal qualification. In his will he remembered the daughters of Richard Ingoldsby, esquire, deceased, son of his former patron. Also remembered were Matthias Ward, "Minister of the Gospel" at Aylesbury, and the three daughters of Dr John Luff. Ward was the pastor of the Presbyterian congregation which had been legally constituted under the Toleration Act of 1689; John Luff, Regius Professor of Medicine at Oxford from 1681 until his death in 1698, was the son of the ejected vicar of Aylesbury.[14]

Less is known about the biographies of Thomas's other acquaintances. John Piddington, who together with his wife Hester was a witness to the will, was an

---

14   BRO MS Wills Peculiar 4/34, will of John Wilson, 1712; Foster, *Alumni Oxonienses*; Lipscomb, *History*, vol. 2, pp. 169, 339–40; *Dictionary of National Biography(DNB)*; typed extracts by R.A. Kidd from A.G. Matthews, *Calamy Revised* (1934) in BRO.

apothecary. Apothecaries by this date were no longer merely shopkeepers but were establishing themselves as medical practitioners in their own right and as a result were rising in the social hierarchy. Among the witnesses to the codicil were William Busby, a prominent local lawyer who owned property in Marsh Gibbon but was resident in Aylesbury, and Francis Tyringham, another member of the landed gentry who lived at Cuddington, both of them justices of the peace and so members of the small elite which ruled the county through the court of Quarter Sessions. Thomas's debtors mentioned in the will included two other local squires and J.P.s, Richard Ingoldsby of Waldridge, son of the regicide, and Thomas Ligo, whose family owned property in Stoke Mandeville and who may have been related to Francis Ligo, J.P., who lived in Aylesbury.

Evidence that Thomas had many less important friends and acquaintances comes from the wills which he himself is known to have witnessed between 1688 and 1695. The testators were Richard Bunce, a victualler, Henry Wells, a yeoman from Aston Clinton, Robert Leatherland, a barber, and Ann Buckland, widow. He also undertook to act as overseer of the wills of two other widows, one of whom, Mary Kipping of Wendover, whose husband had been a yeoman, left a pair of gloves to "her loving friend" Thomas Hickman for his trouble – a gift he never received since she outlived him.[15]

A Gentleman of Modest Property

The picture that thus emerges is that of a man of modest property and good social position living in dignified comfort but involved in the wider community and possessing sufficient ready cash to be able to engage in a certain amount of moneylending, the latter being an activity quite commonly engaged in by all classes at this period, often to oblige friends and acquaintances in a period when banks as we know them did not exist.

What is also clear is that Thomas was of local stock and that he had come up in the world, since none of the numerous relations he mentions in his will was of equal status to himself. Intriguingly, too, all his property, including his own house, had been acquired by purchase, the vendor's name being carefully stated in each case. Moreover, most of the Walton property, which was to provide the bulk of the income for the charity, is, unlike the other acquisitions, described as having been "lately purchased" from a certain Thomas Deering. The word "lately" in such a context is not to be taken too literally, but in this instance it was accurate for a

---

15 Attwood, "Abstract of Registered Wills"; BRO D/A/We/47/45, will of Mary Kipping, 1702 (made 1693).

stray document relating to the conveyance in question has been traced and it is dated Michaelmas 1695, only a few months before the will was drawn up.[16]

So how had Thomas Hickman acquired his affluence and his status, such as they were? Was he, like his younger and much wealthier contemporary, William Mead, who rebuilt the nearby Prebendal House and grammar school not long after Thomas's death, a retired London merchant? Or had he prospered in one of the professions, either in Aylesbury itself or elsewhere?

Schoolmaster and Parish Officer

No evidence has been found of a Thomas Hickman practising medicine or law locally and indeed the evidence of the will itself with its lack of legal rigour argues against his having been a lawyer. On the other hand, a certain Thomas Hickman, together with one Charles Baggaly, clerk (i.e. clergyman), is recorded as having appeared at ecclesiastical visitations held for Aylesbury in November 1669 and again in June 1673 and on each occasion produced his schoolmaster's licence from the church authorities. Baggaly is probably the Charles Bagley (or Baggaley) who graduated B.A. from Christ Church College, Oxford, in 1662; Hickman's name does not appear as a graduate of either university.[17]

The surviving administrative records of the parish of Aylesbury and of the county court of Quarter Sessions contain references to only two persons called Thomas Hickman at this period, one of whom is distinguished as "Junior", prior to 1682, when the burial of the other is recorded in the parish register. Thomas, junior, if – as seems likely – he is our Thomas, is probably the Thomas, who was baptised in 1637, son of Thomas Hickman (henceforth Thomas, senior).[18] Although thus too young to have fought in the Civil War of 1642–6, his early life would have been overshadowed by the dramatic events of that era, when Aylesbury was an important front-line garrison for the parliamentary forces. He would have been only five at the outbreak of the conflict, eleven when the king was executed in 1649 and a young man of twenty-three when Charles II was restored to his throne in 1660. He first appears in the parish records at the age of 33 in 1670

---

16   BRO D/X 68/48.

17   BRO MS Archd. pprs Bucks. c. 301, act book containing triennial visitations of Lincoln peculiars in Bucks and Berks (this is the only volume of its kind extant); Foster, *Alumni Oxonienses.* No schoolmaster's licence for Thomas Hickman is included in the lists of licences in the Lincoln diocesan archives (information kindly supplied by the staff of Lincolnshire Archives).

18   BRO PR 11/1/1, Aylesbury parish register. Unless otherwise indicated, genealogical information given is taken directly or indirectly from parish registers in BRO. Baptismal entries normally give the father's name only at this period, but see also chapter 3 for Thomas Hickman's parentage.

when he served as one of the four, annually-appointed, parish overseers of the poor and the Sessions records show that he was a parish constable in 1683–4.[19]

The overseers' account book covering 1670, the year of Thomas Hickman's appointment, still survives. The accounts for that year, which come first in the volume, are unique in having outsize headings in a fine calligraphic script, with large capitals decorated in elaborate and intricate scrollwork. It looks like the sort of script that might have been produced by a professional penman. Could it, perhaps, have been written by Thomas Hickman himself? The answer is yes, judging by his bold, well-formed signature witnessing the will of Francis Claydon of Bishopstone, father of Joseph Claydon, the trustee, written in June 1696 and those on other surviving original wills which he witnessed. In particular the capital "H" in the signatures has distinctive whorls which resemble those of the same letter as rendered in the 1670 accounts, though much less extravagantly written. The identification becomes a virtual certainty with the discovery in the account book of another signature dated April 1680 – in which, uniquely, the first name is not abbreviated – among those of five leading townsmen who audited the previous year's accounts which is intermediate in style between the 1670 heading and the later version of Thomas Hickman's signature.[20] Thus even without further corroboration there seems no reason to doubt that Thomas Hickman the sometime constable and overseer, Thomas Hickman the schoolmaster and Thomas Hickman the testator were one and the same person.

A Writing Master?

Aylesbury's only public educational establishment at this time was the free grammar school, founded in 1598, which was then accommodated in a room within the parish church. It had about twenty pupils in 1709. But it seems unlikely that Thomas Hickman was ever employed there since the endowment – a mere £8 a year, besides a house for the master – was insufficient of itself to support even one schoolmaster, let alone the two or more that one might have expected to find. In the circumstances it was inevitable that the single appointment would have been held by a clergyman of the Church of England. Most grammar school heads at the time were in holy orders, for clergymen, being almost invariably graduates themselves, were equipped to teach the classical Latin curriculum, designed to prepare boys for university, to which such schools were committed. Equally important, they were also in a position to supplement an inadequate income by doubling as

---

19 BRO PR 11/12/2, overseers' accounts, 1670–83; W. Le Hardy (ed.), *Bucks Sessions Records*, vol. 1 (Aylesbury 1933), p. 148.
20 BRO D/A/Wf/58/79; PR 11/12/2.

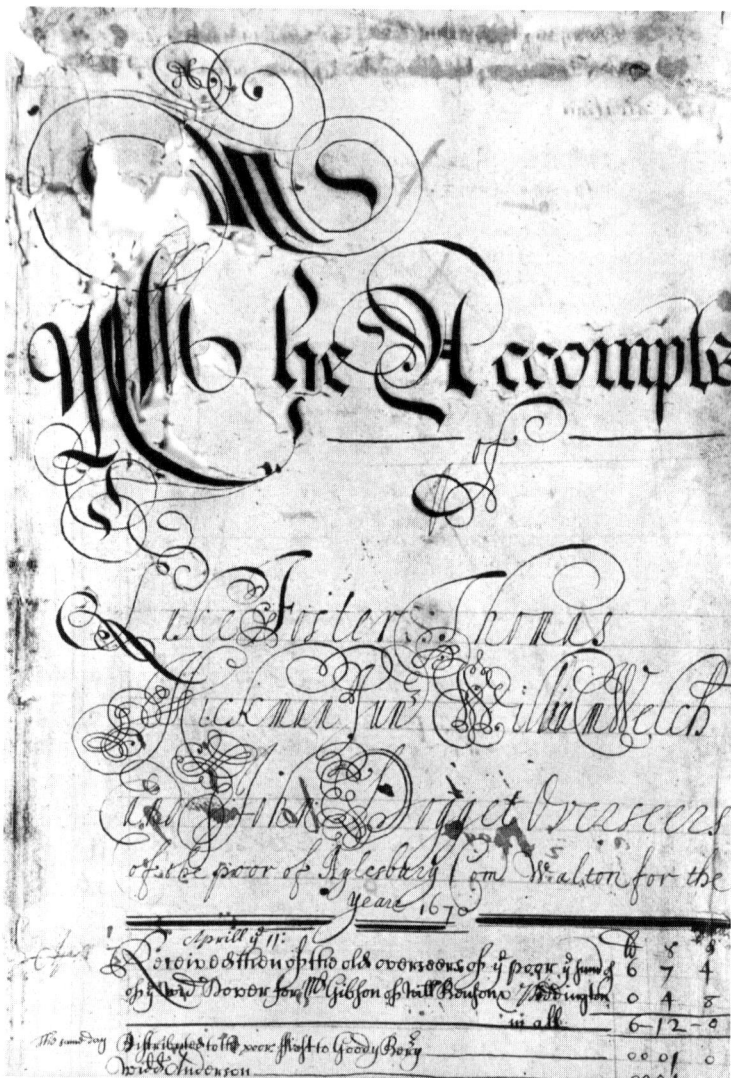

At the age of 33, Thomas Hickman was appointed an overseer of the poor and almost certainly wrote the heading to the first page of the accounts for the year 1670, shown here. The elaborate flourishes (known technically as "command of hand") demonstrate considerable skill in penmanship and the distinctive whorls of the capital "H" resemble those of his signature.

The signatures of Thomas Hickman (above) in 1680 approving the parish overseers' accounts and (below) in 1696 as a witness to the will of Francis Claydon. Compare with the heading to the 1670 accounts on p. 14

vicars or curates. Thus Ralph Gladman, who was master at Aylesbury by 1689 and was still in post in 1709, was curate of Stoke Mandeville and in addition was allowed to charge fees. [21]

Where then did Thomas Hickman, the schoolmaster, fit into the educational scheme of things? We can only speculate, but one possibility, which the known facts seem to support, is that he was a freelance writing master. Writing was not normally taught in the so-called "petty", i.e. elementary, schools, nor was it part of the regular curriculum of the grammar schools either. This gap had come to be filled by specialist writing masters, successors in terms of their art to the medieval scribes, some of whom taught as many as twelve different hands. Examples of their virtuosity can be found in the many published copybooks such as that

21 John Broad (ed.), *Buckinghamshire Dissent and Parish Life 1669–1712* (Buckinghamshire Record Society, vol. 28, 1993), pp.222, 227. *Bucks Sessions Records*, vol. 1, p.292; W. R. Mead, *Aylesbury Grammar School 1598–1998* (Aylesbury, 1998).

produced by Edward Cocker (1631–1675), writing master and arithmetician, in 1657, which includes a specimen script that has affinities with Thomas Hickman's own. Nearer to home, Thomas Watson, who kept a writing school – otherwise unrecorded – at Newport Pagnell, published a copy book in 1683 which offered "the most Usefull & Modish Hands ... Composed of diverse New devised Knots and beautified with many other Curious Shapes & Florishes Fitted for the Profit and Delight of Ingenious Youth". As time went on, however, the emphasis was less on calligraphy as such and more on the plain, legible round hand that became the norm in the eighteenth century, a development which eventually had the effect of devaluing the writing master's special expertise.

Like Cocker, most writing masters also taught arithmetic and some offered accounting and even mathematics and surveying as well, practical subjects for which there was a rising demand in an increasingly commercial

A London writing master's trade card, *c.* 1690. A good example of the entrepreneurial approach adopted by professional writing instructors. Note that Arithmetic was also taught.

society but which the endowed grammar schools of the time were for the most part unable or unwilling to provide. Writing masters were often itinerant, but in larger market towns it was apparently quite usual to find a private fee-paying writing-school alongside the local grammar school, which the grammar-school boys, and others, attended by arrangement. This, one assumes, is the kind of school that Thomas Hickman may have taught. Two years after Thomas's death a settlement certificate among the parish records attests the arrival in 1702 from Thame, in Oxfordshire, of Thomas Hill, "writing master", evidence that the services of such practitioners were in demand locally at this period. After 1714 the situation altered following the lavish re-endowment of the free grammar school in that year, since the new statutes made provision for a designated writing master to teach writing, arithmetic and accounts for the benefit of boys not aspiring to a

Frontispiece of copy book published by Thomas Watson, teacher of a writing school at Newport Pagnell, Buckinghamshire, and others, 1683. The great majority of known copy books are the work of London-based writing masters, some of whose careers are well documented. In contrast, relatively little is known about their provincial counterparts.

classical education. Interestingly, the salary paid (£40 a year, with an extra £5 for keeping the trustees' accounts) was on a par with that of the Latin master.[22]

Evidence from other places suggests that in a bustling market town like Aylesbury, with a population of around 2,000 in 1700, a successful private schoolmaster – like a successful apothecary – could hope to achieve prosperity and respectability through his profession, especially if he took in boarders. In addition Thomas Hickman may have inherited something from his father, even though the latter was clearly not a rich man.

Although the authors of the published copy books were intent on projecting an image of themselves as men of learning and culture, very little is in fact known about the background and training of the average writing master, but some of them are known to have served formal apprenticeships. If this indeed is what he was, Thomas may well have begun his career by attending the free grammar school and then gone elsewhere to acquire his skills. As we shall see, there is reason to think that he was not living in Aylesbury in 1660 and it may well be that much of the earlier part of his life prior to his reappearance in the records in 1669 was spent away from the town.

As far as acquisition of property is concerned, Thomas Hickman ostensibly did not occupy any property in 1673 as he is not included in the extant tax assessment of that year, but his name can just be discerned there in the cancelled portion of a corrected entry for "Mr Thomas Dawson". Since, according to his will, it was from Thomas Dawson that Thomas purchased No. 1 Church Street it is a reasonable inference that he already had an interest of some kind in the property at this date, perhaps as part-occupier or as informal tenant. There is evidence, too, to indicate that the cottages adjoining the churchyard were in Thomas's possession by 1682 (the year Thomas, senior, died), for in the following year the overseers of the poor made two payments to Thomas Hickman, the first of which is dated January 1683 (1682 Old Style) for rent due from one Andrew Hill.[23] At this time the parish authorities regularly provided rent relief for the poor and although there is a gap in the accounts between 1683 and 1697, it seems probable that the payments continued, for one of the tenants of the church gate cottages named in the will was "Widow Hill" and Andrew Hill is known from the parish register to have drowned himself in a well ("his own well") in 1694.

---

22   *DNB*; BRO PR 11/13/31/21(Thomas Hill); Mead, *Aylesbury Grammar School*, pp. 10–15. The principal non-local secondary sources consulted for this and following paragraphs were: W.A.L. Vincent, *The Grammar Schools…1660–1714* (1969); Geoffrey Holmes, *Augustan England. Professions, State and Society 1680–1730* (1982); Rosemary O'Day, *Education and Society 1500–1800* (1982); Ambrose Heal, *The English-Writing Masters and their Copy-Books 1570–1800* (1931) Joyce Irene Whalley and Vera C. Kaden, *The Universal Penman* (HMSO, 1980).

23   BRO PR 11/12/2; for Dawson see Appendix C.

An Election Dispute

Although so little is known about him personally, there is one piece of evidence that Thomas Hickman did not keep entirely aloof from the turbulent politics of the day. In Aylesbury these were characterised by fiercely-contested borough elections between the Whigs, the political successors of the Roundheads of the Civil War, and the Tories, who were pre-eminently the Church of England party. Prior to 1680 the Whigs, under the leadership of Lee and Ingoldsby, had had things all their own way – for the former parliamentary garrison could still be described as a "fanatic" place – but since then the situation had become more fluid and in the mid-1690s every vote counted. No holds were barred in these contests and numerous petitions by defeated candidates alleging bribery and other irregularities came before committees of the House of Commons, themselves not renowned for their impartiality. At the hearing of a petition against the election of James Herbert, the Tory candidate, in October 1695 evidence was given:

Value for money. In January 1696, before a committee of the House of Commons, Thomas Hickman denied promising to pay Giles Reed if he would vote for James Herbert, the Tory parliamentary candidate. Two silver crown coins like this of William III would have paid the alleged bribe, and were as much as a farm labourer earned in fifteen days at local rates.

> That Tho. Hickman asked Giles Reed to be for Mr Herbert; upon which Reed told him, that there was 10s. due to him since the last Election; and, if Mr. Herbert did not pay it him, he would not be for him; whereupon Hickman promised to pay him the said 10s. and that Reed voted for Mr. Herbert; but [the witnesses] could not say, whether the 10s. was paid him.[24]

Although both Hickman and Reed denied any wrongdoing, it is obvious that Thomas was on the Tory side. This is perhaps a little surprising in view of his

24 *Journal of the House of Commons*, vol. xi, p.418 (28 Jan. 1695/6). For the political situation in Aylesbury see Basil Duke Henning, *The History of Parliament. The House of Commons 1660–1690*, vol. 1 (1983), pp. 138–9.

friendship with the old Puritan, John Wilson, but considerations of expediency may have played a part since, as has been seen, schoolmasters needed to be licensed by the Church; in any case friendships that crossed the political divide were by no means unknown. Thomas's acquaintances the Piddingtons were also involved in the proceedings, Mrs Piddington having allegedly prevailed upon one elector to transfer his vote to Herbert by promising him one of her husband's coats, though not until he had finished wearing it! As apothecary to the county jail, then located in the market place, Piddington depended on the good will of the political party in power; not surprisingly, when the Whigs returned to office the following year his services were no longer required and his place was taken by a rival apothecary.

The consequences of the 1695 dispute were to be more than usually significant for it was on this occasion that the House resolved (in January 1696) that the right of election in the borough of Aylesbury lay in all the householders who were not in receipt of alms, a definition which remained the standard one locally thereafter.

3

The Hickmans in Aylesbury 1592–1700

The 1696 Legatees

With the possible exception of the first, the beneficiaries of the five large legacies of £100 (a sum equivalent to more than twice the annual income of the average vicar) which Thomas Hickman charged upon his estate were all relations on his father's side of the family. They were (in the order in which they were to be paid):

1. Mary Day ("cousin"), if then living. She was to receive the interest of the legacy for life and after her death the capital was to go to her son Charles Withers. Neither Mary Day nor her son have been identified.
2. Joseph Hickman ("cousin") and his three children (not named), the money to be divided amongst them, £20 at a time. Joseph was the father of Robert, the trustee; one of his children died before the will was proved.
3. Elizabeth, Sarah and Mary, the three daughters of the testator's deceased cousin William Hickman; the money to be divided equally.
4. The children and grandchildren then living of the late Elizabeth Nelson, eldest daughter of the testator's late uncle Robert Hickman.
5. The children of the late Mary Humphrey, Uncle Robert's youngest daughter.

In contrast, the recipients of the small pecuniary legacies, totalling probably no more than £10 between them, can all, apart from Francis Claydon and his children, be identified as members of the Plater family of Haddenham. They are Faith's sister Grace Brown and her brother John Plater, the trustee, and their respective children and the children of Richard Jarvis and of Cousin Munday, both deceased, who can be identified as the husbands of Faith's aunts Elizabeth Jervice and Alice Munday.

Uncle Robert is the closest relation mentioned in the will and the information concerning him in legacy no. 4 and legacy no. 5 above is the firmest foundation for reconstructing the founder's immediate family background. This information is consistent only with the Robert Hickman who, according to the parish register, married Elizabeth Newman in 1630 and died in 1672. One daughter, Elizabeth, was born in 1640 and another, Mary, in 1650. Elizabeth's marriage (to a man named Nelson) has not been traced, but Mary is presumably the Mary Hickman who married Joseph Humphrey in 1675. Uncle Robert was also the father of Cousin Joseph, mentioned in legacy no. 2 – whose baptism is said to have been recorded in a family bible – and thus the grandfather of Robert, the trustee. All three are known to have been carpenters. Cousin William, mentioned in legacy no. 3, is almost certainly Uncle Robert's second son of that name, who died in 1688. Two of William's children by his second wife were Sarah, born in 1677, and Mary, born in 1678. No daughter called Elizabeth has been traced, but the second marriage did not take place in Aylesbury and William may have been living elsewhere for a time before 1677. He too is known to have been a carpenter.[25]

The Early Seventeenth Century

At this point it may be useful to attempt to reconstruct the history of the Hickmans in Aylesbury using the parish register and such other contemporary sources as can be found. In the virtual absence of wills and other family documents the results are necessarily somewhat tentative and there are many loose ends. The difficulties are compounded by the frequent duplication of Christian names and by possible under-registration, especially during the Civil War period of the 1640s, when the parish registers are clearly incomplete. Partly for these reasons, this chapter is best read with the help of the pedigrees in Figs. 1 and 2 (pages 33 & 34).

The Hickman family was established in Buckinghamshire by the early sixteenth century, if not before, notably in Great Missenden and Linslade (now in Bedfordshire) where several of them are listed in a county muster roll of 1522. They first appear in the Aylesbury parish register – which begins in 1564 – in 1592, when the burial of one Agnes Hickman is entered, and thereafter they occur fairly continuously from 1608. Between those two dates a stray Hickman reference in a different source may provide a clue to the family's antecedents. In his will, made in April 1603, Robert Alexander of Aylesbury, yeoman, left a small legacy of

---

25 Lipscomb, *History,* vol. 2, p. 52; *Bucks Sessions Records,* vol. 1, p.141. Lipscomb, *History,* vol. 2, p. 52, uniquely cites "Family bible" as his source for the (correctly stated) baptismal date of Joseph Hickman, son of Robert, in 1637.

five shillings to a certain Jacquement Hickman. This very unusual Christian name recurs in the will of Elizabeth Hickman of Southcott in Linslade, made the same year, in reference to one of her four unmarried daughters. Here then is an apparent link. Further investigation discloses that the Southcott Hickmans were related to the Gurney family of Aylesbury and that in the late sixteenth century both had an interest in the same copyhold property at Broughton in Bierton parish. Beyond this, however, the evidence found does not allow us to go and we accordingly return to the Aylesbury parish register.[26]

This tells us that in February 1609 Robert Hickman married Dorothy Cockman, second daughter of William Cockman, yeoman, a member of one of Aylesbury's leading families. Since several Cockmans held the office of bailiff of the manor of Aylesbury and one, William Cockman, who died in 1589, was the donor of the almshouses to which reference is made in chapter 1, it follows that Robert must have been a man of some consequence, but nothing is known about him beyond the baptism of a son, William, in 1609 and of three daughters between 1612 and 1617, when Robert's own burial is recorded. Dorothy Hickman's burial follows in 1623, after which Robert Hickman's family disappears from the records and its relationship to other Aylesbury Hickmans remains obscure.

Robert was not the only male Hickman to appear in Aylesbury around this time, for in 1609 and 1611 Agnes and Thomas, the children of one William Hickman, were baptised and baptisms of two more children followed, Cicely in 1614 and Henry, who lived for a few days only, in 1616. William probably came to Aylesbury from Stoke Mandeville where the baptisms of Robert and John, sons of William Hickman, are recorded in 1605 and 1606 respectively.[27] This conjecture is strengthened by the burial entry in the Aylesbury register in 1619 of John, son of William Hickman, for whom no previous baptism had been recorded. John's two surviving male siblings, Thomas and Robert, were probably the founder's father, Thomas, senior, and his uncle Robert; there are no other likely candidates. William's wife Sybil died in 1626; he himself evidently survived until 1637, when there is a burial entry for "William Hickman the old man".

In 1614 a third Hickman family was inaugurated in Aylesbury by the marriage of another William Hickman to Jane, only daughter of John Keble, or Keeble, of Aylesbury, gentleman, deceased. William II's relationship to his namesake is

---

26   A. C. Chibnall (ed.), *The Certificate of Musters for Buckinghamshire in 1522* (Bucks Record Society, vol. 17, 1973); Buckinghamshire Archaeological Society, F.G. Gurney notebooks, GUR/NB/books v, x.
27   BRO AR 131/81, Bishop's transcripts of parish registers, Stoke Mandeville (typed transcript in BRO).

unknown, but we know that he was related in some way to Thomas Hickman the founder. Although both parties were described as "of Aylesbury", the marriage actually took place at Princes Risborough.[28] It was clearly a clandestine, or runaway, union, a circumstance which is most readily explained by the differences in the couple's wealth and status, for the bridegroom was a carpenter by trade, whereas the bride was the daughter of a self-styled gentleman who had left property to her in her own right. John Keble had accumulated a small urban estate as a result of various property transactions, both freehold and leasehold, from the 1560s onward.[29] When he died in 1603 he left most of his property to his wife Dorothy for her lifetime, together with the guardianship of their two under-age children, John and Jane, who each received separate bequests of property of their own. Keble's will also stipulated that if both children should die young and unmarried the estate should be used to endow the wages of a schoolmaster "in the teaching and training up in learning of the children of the poorer sort."[30]

William II (or William, junior, as he is usually styled in the register until 1623) and his wife Jane had some eight children between 1616 and 1627. Unluckily for them they were all girls requiring dowries if they were to have a proper start in life. Despite this William was among the minority of the population wealthy enough to pay the national tax of 1626 and he held the important office of churchwarden in 1639. He was still living in 1642 when he contributed 2s. 6d. – an amount well above the average – to the voluntary fund for the relief of the distressed Irish Protestants.[31]

Although no burial is recorded, William II was dead by October 1648, when his widow Jane sold a house beside the market place, part of the property left to her by her father, to Henry and Ann Monday for the then very large sum of £240. Two of the witnesses to this transaction, of which only a copy survives, were Jane's son-in-law Francis Claydon, father of Joseph Claydon the trustee and "kinsman" of 1696, who had married Jane's daughter Martha in 1641, and Thomas Hickman, who is almost certainly Thomas, senior, the founder's father. A third witness was Robert Leatherland, a name that recurs in the list of wills witnessed by the founder over forty years later (see p. 11). Here we have evidence of close links between these two branches of the Hickmans. The names of Francis and Thomas had earlier been associated in connection with the will, made in 1644, of Thomas

28   BRO PR 175/1/1.

29   H. A. Hanley, " 'A Singular Commodity' … Bedford's Charity, Aylesbury, 1494–1597", in *Records of Buckinghamshire*, vol. 35 (1995, for 1993), p. 60.

30   BRO D/A/We/22/65.

31   John Wilson (ed.), *Buckinghamshire Contributions for Ireland 1642* … (Bucks Record Society, vol. 21, 1983), p. 82.

Fountain of Walton, Francis in the capacity of an overseer of the will and Thomas as an appraiser of the probate inventory of the deceased's goods. [32]

Thomas, Senior, and Uncle Robert

After this nothing more is heard of Jane and her other daughters, all of whom would have been grown up by 1648. Meanwhile Robert and Thomas, the presumed sons of the first William Hickman, had both set up house. Uncle Robert's wife, Elizabeth, whom he married in November 1630, was the daughter of Henry Newman of Aylesbury, yeoman. Her father had made his will a few months earlier leaving her £12, payable within a year or on marriage and she had lost no time in claiming it.[33] Altogether, Uncle Robert and Elizabeth had more than eight children between 1631 and 1652, four of whom were sons. In 1655 there is a glimpse of Robert in his professional role when he is named an arbitrator, together with William Clarke, a mason, in a dispute concerning the chimney of a house in what is now Temple Street and in the 1660s he is found attesting the parish overseers' accounts on several occasions. From the mid-1650s, if not earlier, Robert was renting two tenements, or houses, on the north side of Castle Street from the lord of the manor, at first jointly with William Newman. With the help of estate rentals, the descent of this property can be traced from Robert to his third, and last-surviving, son Joseph and his grandson Robert (the trustee of 1696) and there is evidence which indicates that it was still in the possession of his descendants in the 1770s. Estate accounts, too, refer to occasional transactions with Robert's son and grandson in connection with work done or timber supplied between 1688 and 1705.[34]

No record of the marriage of Thomas, senior, has been found prior to the baptism of his son Thomas, the testator, in 1637, but it appears from the poll tax of 1660 that his wife's name was Elizabeth. Three other children, Alice, Jane and Sarah, were baptised in 1639, 1642 and 1646 respectively and the burial of a son, yet another William, whose baptism is not recorded, is entered in 1642. The fate of the sisters is not known. Around 1655 Thomas, senior, was occupying a freehold house in Walton Street, the precise location of which is unknown.[35] In 1642

---

32 BRO BAS Deeds 547/37; BRO D/A/Wf/35/17. Francis Claydon is described as "junior" in Fountain's will to distinguish him from F.C., senior, the other overseer.

33 BRO D/A/Wf/28/22, will of Henry Newman.

34 BRO D/PC/41, deed, 1655; D/X 1007/22/1–20; Birmingham Central Library, Hampton MSS, nos.737–792 (rentals, 1650–1726), 793–801 (estate accounts, 1688–1709); BRO D 1/9/23 (sale particulars, 1778). There is a microfilm copy of the Hampton MSS items in BRO.

35 BRO D/X 1007/22.

A seventeenth-century carpenter at work. From a set of engravings of Arts and Crafts by J. J. Van der Vliet, 1635. Many of the Hickman family in the seventeenth and eighteenth centuries were carpenters, including Joseph, whose letter is shown on p. 30, and his son, Robert, to whom the founder bequeathed his mathematical instruments. These may have included a pair of compasses like the pair shown on the floor in the picture.

Thomas, senior, gave 1s. for the distressed Irish Protestants and his brother Robert 6d.[36] In 1654 Thomas was one of fewer than a hundred electors for the borough whose signatures appear on the official return for the parliamentary election of that year; another of the signatories was Francis Claydon.[37]

According to the poll tax levied following the Restoration of Charles II in 1660, which in theory embraced all resident adults, male and female, there were only two Hickman households in Aylesbury at this date, namely those of Thomas, senior, and his brother Robert. Both paid at the flat rate, which means that neither was in the category of "persons able to dispend" more than £5 per annum (about a third of Aylesbury householders), who were taxed on their lands or goods.[38] Uncle Robert's household comprised himself and Elizabeth his wife, their grown-up second and third sons William and Joseph (the eventual heir), born in 1633 and 1637 respectively, and a servant, William Turnam, who was probably an apprentice or journeyman. In contrast, Thomas, senior, was taxed for himself and Elizabeth his wife only. His son Thomas, the founder, would have been old enough at 23 years to be liable for the tax, so he was probably not living in Aylesbury at this time.

Thomas, senior, survived until 1682; his wife having apparently died some three years earlier. His occupation is unknown, but he was considered rich enough to pay the hearth tax in 1662, though for one hearth only.[39] Because the records of the tax in Bucks are defective, it is not possible to say whether he also paid in 1672, but unlike Uncle Robert and his son Joseph, he is not included in the list (a large proportion of the population) of those exempted from payment on grounds of poverty.[40] A property tax assessment for 1668 lists payments by William, Robert and Thomas Hickman, but a similar assessment for 1673 was paid by William and Robert's widow (he died in 1672) only, even though Thomas, junior, was, as we have seen, an overseer of the poor in 1670.[41]

Uncle Robert's first-born son Robert, born 1631, and his fourth, and youngest, son Thomas, born 1642, do not recur in the records and may be presumed to have died. His second son William (Cousin William of the will) married Judith Thorpe in 1661. Judith bore him two children, William, junior, who died in 1670, and Mary (presumed to have died), before dying herself in 1673. William seems to

36   Wilson, *Bucks Contributions*, p.81.
37   Public Record Office (PRO), Parliamentary Returns 44 (1), 1654 (extracts in *VCH* Notes in BRO).
38   BRO D/LE/17/3.
39   PRO E179/80/348 (damaged and incomplete).
40   PRO E179/324.
41   BRO D/LE/17/8, 9; see also Appendix C.

Wood turner at work. Another print from the same set of engravings as the previous one. Note the pole lathe and unfinished spinning wheel. Joseph Hickman was paid a shilling for supplying such a wheel for the parish in 1697. Joseph, born the same year as his cousin Thomas, the founder, was the ancestor of all the Hickmans born in Aylesbury for over a century.

have remarried by 1676. Reference has already been made to the baptisms of two female children, Sarah and Mary, both born prior to 1682, when the burial of Joan, wife of William Hickman, is recorded, and, as has been seen, another daughter, Elizabeth, is also indicated in the founder's will. Like his father and brother, Cousin William adopted the family trade of carpentry, but he could turn his hand to surveying also for in 1684, the year before he served as a parish constable, he was granted 40s. by the county court of Quarter Sessions "for his pains in surveighing a place for to build a new Gaole [i. e. jail] uppon."[42] He died in 1688.

Cousin Joseph and his Family

Robert's third son, Cousin Joseph, born the same year as the founder and still living in 1696, had six children by his marriage to Susan, or Susanna, daughter of William Hurndall of Wing, yeoman, in 1669. Only three – Robert, the trustee named in the founder's will, who was baptised in 1670, Susannah, baptised in 1672, and Joseph, baptised in 1674 – survived infancy.[43] In 1683 Joseph took over the tenancy of an unspecified property belonging to the Bedford Charity estate, for which he paid a rent of 14s. a year – equivalent to an acre or two of land. The previous tenant had been "Widow Hickman", almost certainly his mother – for the burial of an Elizabeth Hickman is recorded in 1682 – and the tenancy may well have been held by his father before her, but the existing record only covers the three years 1682–4. During the same period he himself supplied the Bedford trustees with posts and rails, for which he charged 6s. 6d. At some time during the late 1680s or 1690s Joseph built, or renovated, a public house or shop for Samuel Very of Wendover, flax dresser and entrepreneur, and it would appear that his turnery skills extended to making a spinning wheel, since the overseers' accounts show that he was paid a shilling for supplying one to the parish in 1697.[44]

Our evidence for the work done for Very is a note from Joseph to his employer (who was also his first cousin on his mother's side of the family) which is among some business correspondence of Very's discovered under the floor boards of a house in Wendover in 1944. As it is the only such composition by any member of the family that has come to light it seems worth reproducing in full and as written. The spelling and punctuation leave something to be desired and the quality of the

---

42 *Bucks Sessions Records,* vol. 1, pp. 141, 182.
43 BRO PR 11/1/1 (the bride's name is given as Hurland in the register, Hurndall in the corresponding Bishop's Transcript); D/A/Wf/53/65, will of William Hurndall, 1685/6 (leaves £20 to J. H., "son-in-law", and his wife, unnamed).
44 BRO BAS185/24, John Wigson's Book (copy accounts of Bedford's Charity, 1682–4); D 4/19/15, Very correspondence, 1684–1701; PR11/12/3.

Undated letter from Joseph Hickman (1637–1699), the founder's cousin, to Samuel Very at Wendover. This is the only known piece of correspondence by a contemporary member of Thomas Hickman's family.

handwriting compares most unfavourably with that of his cousin Thomas, but the reference to two expected bottles of wine shows that Joseph had an appreciation of the finer things in life.

Cusen very this is to let you know that I have dune that which you ordered all but The sine [sign] For he will not have a gibbet [i. e. hanging] sine so I intend to let all alone till you come over your self[.] hee would have mee make foure new doores Till you come over and hee will see me paid for them[.] Cusen you promised to send over two bottels of old maligoe [Malaga, a white Spanish wine] but I am afraid you have for got[.] my son thought [it] long till Satterday come[.] pray If you have [forgot?] send for some this weeke with out faile for wee have left the dooer in hopes you would have sente it to day so no more at present[.] I rest your lovein kinsman[,]

Feb[.] the 18

                                                        Joseph Hickman

The Platers

The Plater family, who figure so largely in the will, were descended from a long line of Haddenham yeomen and husbandmen (see Fig. 2). They do not appear to have been particularly prosperous. Unlike the Hickmans, they are documented by a series of wills beginning in 1544, none of which, however, directly alludes to the kinship with the Hickmans. This connection seems to have originated in 1615, when Richard Plater, grandfather of John Plater, the trustee, married Katherine Hickman in the adjoining parish of Aston Sandford. Precisely how Katherine Hickman was related to the Aylesbury Hickmans is not known, but she was evidently part of the same extended family. When grandfather Richard died in 1669, he left a token 12d. apiece to his daughters Alice Munday and Elizabeth Jervice, both indicated in Thomas Hickman's will, and 20s. to each of their children.[45]

Richard's son John, father of the trustee, is probably the John Plater of Haddenham whose wife and children were reported to be unbaptised in a return of religious Nonconformists in 1669, for the parish registers contain few references to the family. Moreover his wife's name, Grace, and those of two of their children were of the kind favoured by Puritans. In his will proved in 1704, he listed three sons and six married daughters, the latter receiving legacies varying between 1s. and £5.[46] Three of the six, Grace Brown, Faith Hitchenden (by the name of Faith Plater, one of the executors) and Katherine Staddar (by the name of Katherine Plater), are also mentioned in Thomas Hickman's will. Faith Plater, then in her late thirties, had married Matthew Hitchenden of Aylesbury in July 1697, after Thomas had drawn up his will but before his deathbed codicil. It is intriguing to note that Matthew's first wife had died only four months previously leaving him a childless widower. He had a particular reason for haste in marrying, however, as he had been left a house in 1681 which would revert to his brother if he had no legitimate children (he was rumoured to have illegitimate ones). In the event he had a daughter, born in 1698, by his new wife and called Faith after her.[47]

The Claydons

The Claydon, or Cleydon, family of Bishopstone in the parish of Stone is less well documented than the Platers. Francis Claydon of Bishopstone, yeoman, whose will the founder witnessed in 1696, married Martha Hickman, presumed to have

---

45   BRO D/A/Wf/45/186.
46   Broad, *Buckinghamshire Dissent*, p. 43; BRO D/A/We/48/46.
47   BRO Library box file 20, MS pedigree of Hitchenden by V. Pether.

been William and Jane's daughter of that name, at Hulcott in 1641. His presence in Hulcott may well have been connected with the Fountain family, who were lords of the manor there around this time, for as noted earlier he was named as one of the overseers (the other was Francis Claydon, senior) of the will of Thomas Fountain in 1644. Four of his children were baptised in Aylesbury between 1645 and 1654, the last being his son Joseph, the trustee, and he was a signatory of the return for the 1654 borough election.[48] By 1659 the baptisms of children of Francis Claydon had begun to be recorded in the Stone parish register. He died in December 1697.

48   See note 37 above.

Robert Hickman = Dorothy Cockman
(d. 1617)   (m. 1609, d.1623)

William (b. 1609)   Other female issue

...

William Hickman I = Sybil
(d. 1637)   (d. 1626)

Robert* = Elizabeth Newman   John (1606-19)   Thomas = Elizabeth   Others (d. yng)
.(1605-72) (m. 1630, d. 1682)   (1611-82) (d. 1679)

THOMAS (1637-98)   Other issue

Elizabeth* = [Nelson] (b. 1640)
Mary* = Joseph Humphrey (b. 1650, m. 1675)

Judith Thorpe = (1)William* = (2)?Joan   Joseph* (1637-99) = Susan Hurndall
(m. 1661)   (1633-88)   (d. 1682)   (m. 1669)

Robert (b. 1631)
Thomas (b. 1642)

[Elizabeth*]
Sarah* (b. 1677)
Mary* (b. 1678)

1 s., (d.1670)
1 dau., d.yng)

William Hickman II = Jane Keble
(d. by 1648)   (m. 1614)

Martha = Francis Claydon   Other female issue
(b. 1619,m. 1641) (d. 1697)

Joseph Claydon (d. 1724)
Trustee & "kinsman"

Joseph (1674-99)

Robert (1670-1746)   Susannah = [John Humphrey]
See Fig.3.   (b. 1672)

Susan   Mary

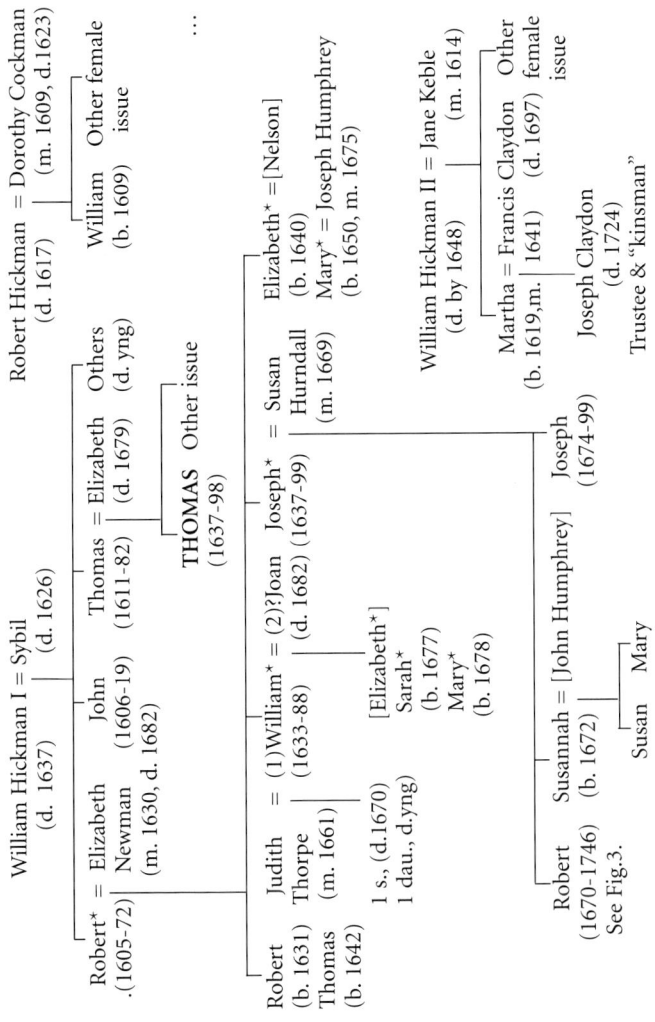

Fig. 1 Pedigree (partly conjectural) of Aylesbury Hickmans to 1700 showing family connections of Thomas Hickman, the founder.

Note. Asterisk against a name indicates that it is mentioned in the founder's will. Square brackets indicates that the name/event was not traced in the parish register.

Richard Plater = Katherine Hickman
  (d. 1669) | (m. 1615 at Aston Sandford)
          ┌──────────┴──────────┐
    John = Grace   Alice = Munday*   Elizabeth = [Richard] Jervice*
    (d. 1704)
┌──────┬──────────┬──────────┬──────────────┬──────────┐
John* Grace* = Brown Faith* = Matthew Katherine*= Staddar Thomas
(d. 1722)   (m. 1697) Hitchenden   Richard
Trustee & "kinsman"   Hester = Stone
                                                              Mary = Hummett
                                                              Elizabeth = Chapman

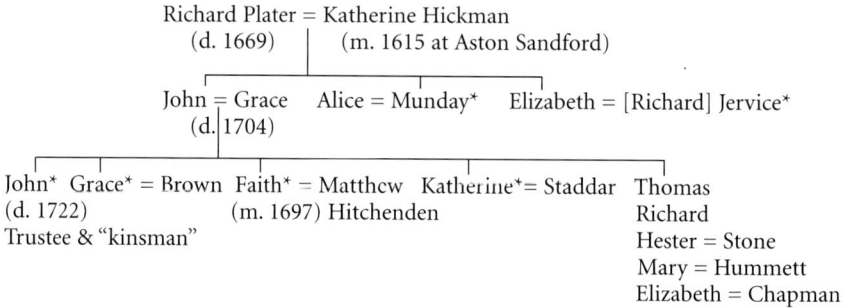

Fig. 2. Pedigree of Plater family of Haddenham, related to Hickman, based on family wills.

Note. Asterisk against a name indicates that it is mentioned in the founder's will.

4

Trusteeship by Inheritance 1698–1760

From the outset, the Hickman family and Thomas Hickman's Charity were intimately intertwined. Robert Hickman, carpenter's son but also himself a carpenter, the first-named of the initial trustees of the charity and the first trustee to bear the family name, was a young man in his late twenties in 1698 when the founder died. Robert's father, Joseph, died in July of the following year, less than two weeks before probate of the founders's will was granted. His younger brother, another Joseph, had predeceased his father by a few months, leaving Robert the only known living male descendant of William Hickman I. By his will Joseph left his share of the £100 legacy from Thomas Hickman, together with all his household goods, to be equally divided between Robert and his sister Susannah, who had married John Humphrey. Legacies of 20s. apiece were left to Joseph's three young grandchildren, Joseph Hickman, and Susan and Mary Humphrey. As would be natural in a family carpentry business, his stock of timber and boards and all his firewood and working tools, together with his clothes and other effects, went to Robert, who was named executor.[49]

This initial trustee, Robert, was destined to be the ancestor of all the Hickmans born in Aylesbury in the following century and more (see Figs. 3 and 4). He had two surviving children by his first wife, Mary Thorne – Joseph, junior, born in 1694, and Robert, junior, born in 1702 – and two more – Thomas, born in 1713, and William, born in 1716 – by his second wife, Ann, whose maiden name is unknown. Three of the four sons – Joseph, Robert and William – married and had families, constituting what may for convenience be termed respectively the senior, middle and junior branches of Robert, the trustee's, family. The senior branch was to provide the family trustees in the early period, but as none of Joseph's Aylesbury-born children

---

49 BRO D/A/We/45/170.

married, it effectively died out early in the following century. Robert, junior, head of the middle branch, had one son and one daughter, both of whom married, but thereafter the middle branch descended in the female line only. This middle branch was downwardly mobile and in time it came to be a fertile source of inmates for the almshouses. In contrast, the junior branch, founded by the youngest son William, was both prolific and upwardly mobile and eventually replaced the senior in the control of the family charity.

Robert Hickman, Trustee, 1698–1747

No trust records are known to have been kept by Robert, the initial trustee, and none whatsoever survive for the eighteenth century, but as the senior representative of the family and the only trustee resident in Aylesbury, he must inevitably have assumed responsibility for the management of the Charity. It is likely that during the first quarter of the eighteenth century there were few if any founder's kin among the occupants of the almshouses, if only because of the generous legacies which so many of them had received under Thomas Hickman's will. Certainly the number of potential Hickman claimants among the three Aylesbury branches remained small until a generation after 1700. Whether the annual distribution to the poor was regularly kept up there is no means of knowing.

Robert, the initial trustee, outlived both his two co-trustees by many years, John Plater dying in 1722 and Joseph Claydon in 1724.[50] It seems likely that the vacancies were not filled and that after 1724 Robert acted alone.

The one certainty about Robert's period as trustee is that No. 1 Church Street, Thomas Hickman's old house, was renovated in 1739, acquiring the fashionable – though asymmetrical – Georgian brick front and handsome pedimented doorcase that distinguish it today.[51] At the same time extra room was created by the insertion of an attic floor, with connecting servants' back staircase, the ground-floor entrance to which is now concealed in a cupboard, and a short extension to the rear. Several original fittings from this period are still intact, including the front door, with its L-shaped hinges, and one or two interior doors. These improvements would have made the house an eminently suitable residence for a well-to-do professional man like Wilson Williams, the apothecary, who was the occupier in 1753. The cost of the operation would most likely have been financed by means of a building lease for a long term at a reduced rent. This would have had the effect of temporarily diminishing the income available for distribution.

---

50   BRO D/A/We/58/97; D/A/We/60/106.
51   Dating tablet on front of building.

Exterior of No. 1 Church Street, the founder's former residence, seen from Temple Square showing the Georgian facade and doorcase, as re-fronted during the Trusteeship of Robert Hickman in 1739 (pp. 36–37). That date is on the tablet visible above the doorcase.

Although the initiative for the rebuilding may well have come from the lessee, it is not improbable that Robert himself was responsible for the carpentry work on the house. References to his professional activities during this generally prosperous and expanding period of the town's history are occasionally met with in the records. The mathematical instruments he had inherited under the will of his cousin Thomas would have come in useful when he rebuilt the farm house at Walton belonging to the trustees of the recently-founded Harding's charity in 1728–9, for which he was paid over £100.[52] The house, with its brick Georgian facade and tiled roof, still stands opposite the pond. Nine years later, in 1737, he was one of three carpenters who entered into an agreement for laying floors in the new county jail, which formed part of the present County Hall in the market place.[53]

52 Record book of Harding's Charity, c.1719–1754, held at Parrott and Coales.
53 Guy Crouch, "The Building of County Hall", in *Records of Buckinghamshire*, vol. 12 (1927–33), p. x.

In 1723 Robert, together with the vicar and three of the town's most prominent citizens, was nominated as a trustee of Eman's charity under the will of the founder, testimony that he enjoyed a measure of public esteem.[54]

Robert Hickman, the first trustee, died, aged 76, in February 1747. In his will he asked that he should be buried "in a plain way and carried to church by my own servants." The will conveys the impression that Robert, perhaps grown cantankerous with age, was not on the best of terms with his wife and family, with the possible exception of his youngest son. His eldest son Joseph got only "all the debt he owes me for repairing his house and money lent him out of my pocket and all the debts he owes me for goods out of my shop." His third son Thomas, stated to be then living in London (he had been apprenticed in the furniture trade there in 1731), received a legacy of £10. The rest of his goods and chattels were to go to his youngest son William for the purpose of paying off his father's debts. Reference is also made to a bond which the testator had entered into, payable to his wife after his death, and the wish was expressed that she and William should "go on together" (i.e. in the business); but if she refused, William was instructed to sell everything and retain what was left after payment of debts. His wife Ann is not mentioned by name, nor is there any reference to the testator's second son Robert, junior. In the event William did not have to go to the extreme of selling the Castle Street property.[55]

Joseph Hickman, Trustee, 1746–1756

By English law when a trust fails to renew itself the freehold of the trust property is vested in the heirs of the last surviving trustee. This is what seems to have happened on the death of Robert, the initial trustee, for his eldest son Joseph, head of the senior branch, then aged 52, a barber living in Walton Street, is known to have kept accounts for the Charity, beginning in 1746.[56] These accounts were still extant in 1833, but have since disappeared and nothing is known about them except that, like those of his successors, they left much to be desired. It is probable that Joseph was also responsible for appointing new co-trustees. Their existence is known only from the archives of the Sun Fire insurance company which issued a policy in March 1753 in the joint names of Joseph

---

54 Gibbs, *Aylesbury,* p. 469.

55 BRO MS Wills Pec. 5/68; typescript "Abstract of Bucks Apprentices…in London Livery Companies" in BRO (Upholders Company).

56 BRO copy MS index to Bucks policy holders with Sun Fire Insurance Co., 1714–31; *26th Report … Concerning Charities,* p.52.

Hickman, Robert Jemmett and William Shelton, "Trustees of the late Mr Thomas Hickmans Charity."[57] Jemmett, who died, aged 67, in 1779, was a draper; Shelton is probably the William Shelton, senior, a currier, or leather-worker, who died in 1758.[58] Both were prominent local tradesmen. What they had in common was that for the four years prior to 1753 they had been jointly churchwardens of Aylesbury and both had held the office in previous years also. As neither was related to Hickman, their appointment could be regarded as a broadening of the basis of the trusteeship. One suspects that they were recent appointments and that Joseph, looking around for new trustees of sufficient respectability, had lighted upon the outgoing churchwardens. Ironically, in 1758 Jemmett was to be a defendant in a lawsuit for the recovery of parish property![59]

An eighteenth-century barber. This and the illustration on p. 44 are taken from an Ornamental Alphabet of Trades and Occupations, *c.* 1770. Joseph, the eldest son of Robert Hickman, the initial Trustee, was a barber living in Walton Street (p. 38).

The Charity Estate in 1753

Fortunately for us, the Sun Fire insurance policy of 1753 (or rather policies, for there were two of them) covers all the Charity's buildings and gives particulars of their current occupants, their construction and the amount insured for. They were:

    a. A house in Church Street, brick, timber and tiled, in the occupation of Wilson Williams, apothecary. £300.

    (This is clearly Thomas Hickman's old house, which Robert, the initial trustee, had refronted in 1739, and which still bears the Sun Fire plaque

57 Guildhall Library G.L. MS 11936/101, Sun Fire policies 134932–3, 1753. The first of these is for the Market Square property only.
58 Gibbs, *Aylesbury,* p.35; BRO MS Wills Pec. 5/128, will of William Shelton, 1757/8.
59 BRO PR11/5/1.

for policy no. 134933. Williams, a Presbyterian, who died in 1758, was one of a dynasty of Aylesbury apothecaries.)[60]

b. A house near the market house, brick and tiled, occupier Michael Fowler, surgeon and apothecary. £200.

(This is No. 11 Market Square which also formed part of the endowment and whose site remains Charity property today.)

c. Another house in Church Street, brick and tiled, occupier Robert Hickman, carpenter. £100.

(This must be No. 16 Church Street, one of the two larger almshouses, here treated separately from the others; the occupier was Joseph's younger brother, Robert, head of the downwardly-mobile middle branch, who had married Elizabeth Parrott in 1730. References to him in the parish rate book suggest that he had been an almshouse tenant since at least 1741, the first Hickman known to have benefited from the Charity in this way.)

d. Four tenements adjoining each other near the aforesaid house, brick, timber and tiled, occupiers: Robert Livings, tailor; Thomas Asberry, labourer; Sarah Lucas, spinster; and the widow Neale. £100.

(The remaining almshouses; their occupants were presumably admitted on grounds of poverty rather than as founder's kin, though the Asbury family were shortly to be linked by marriage to the Hickmans.)

e. A farm house and adjoining milk house in Walton, brick, timber and tiled, occupier William North, farmer. £100.

Charity and Politics in 1756

Joseph, junior, died in November 1756 without leaving a will. Information about the tenancy of the almshouses at this time can be gleaned from an unusual source – an annotated list of persons voting for Thomas Potter, one of the candidates in a by-election for the borough of Aylesbury held the following month.[61] Nowadays we do not readily associate charities with politics, but in eighteenth-century Aylesbury the case was otherwise. To the aspiring politician they offered a potential cheap source of patronage in the form of employment, contracts, favourable leases and similar "perks". Not for nothing was John Wilkes, the celebrated demagogue, who succeeded his friend Potter as one of Aylesbury's two M.P.s the following year, a trustee of several of the town's larger charities.

But charities had a special political significance in Aylesbury, for as we have

60 Gibbs, *Aylesbury*, p.35.   61 BRO D/AF/263/1.

A closer view of No. 1 Church Street. Details of the elegant classical portico and brick mouldings can be clearly seen.

seen, the right to vote was restricted to householders not receiving alms and so the vote of anyone in receipt of benefit of a charitable nature was liable to be challenged. The list of Potter's voters was evidently compiled on behalf of his defeated opponent. The name of each voter is marked G[ood] or Q[uery], with explanatory comments added in red ink. The following names are queried on account of occupying a "gift house" of Hickman's charity:

> Thomas Asbury
> Thomas Hickman "not [a] parishioner"
> Robt Hickman Senr
> Robert Levings

In addition, the name of Richard Shelton, probably a relation of William Shelton, the new trustee, is queried, with the comment "For an house of Mrs Greens by the church yard Its being Hickmans Charity". The significance of this is obscure and is possibly an error. Three of the names in the above list are those of inmates of the almshouses in 1753, but there was now another Hickman, Thomas, not born in the parish, or not having a legal settlement there. He was presumably Joseph's bachelor step-brother, Thomas, who was living in London at the time of his father's death but is known to have returned to live in Aylesbury. The same names, along with that of Widow Neale, recur in an undated rough sketch map of around 1755–60 showing part of Parsons Fee (see p. 43).[62]

The list of Potter's voters also includes three other Hickman householders not occupying "gift" houses. Two of these are Joseph's youngest brother, William, head of the junior branch, and Joseph's son, Robert, junior, who had just inherited a house from his father. The third was John Hickman, unmarried son of Robert, senior, head of the middle branch, born in 1731, whose name also has a "Q" against it and the comment "A new made vote for a house in Peeble [i.e. Pebble] Lane."

In the list of voters many names are queried on the grounds that their owners had allegedly received charitable distributions of cash; significantly, no distribution on behalf of Hickman's is specified. Confirmation that the annual distribution was being neglected is found in a memorandum concerning parish charities entered at the front of a volume of the churchwardens' accounts for 1749–1787. This states that:

> Hickmans Charity being an estate of £40 per annum ….has in part been applied in the years 1758, 1759 and 1760 in payment of Dawneys and Mr Merricks Rent and the accounts inspected and signed by Mr Bell and Mr Harry Saunders Churchwardens *therefore if that Charity is again or should be lost to the parish it must be egregious neglect in the parish or its officers.*[63]

62 BRO D/X 1200/2.
63 BRO PR 11/5/1; see also abbreviated version in Gibbs, *Aylesbury,* p.391. Italics supplied.

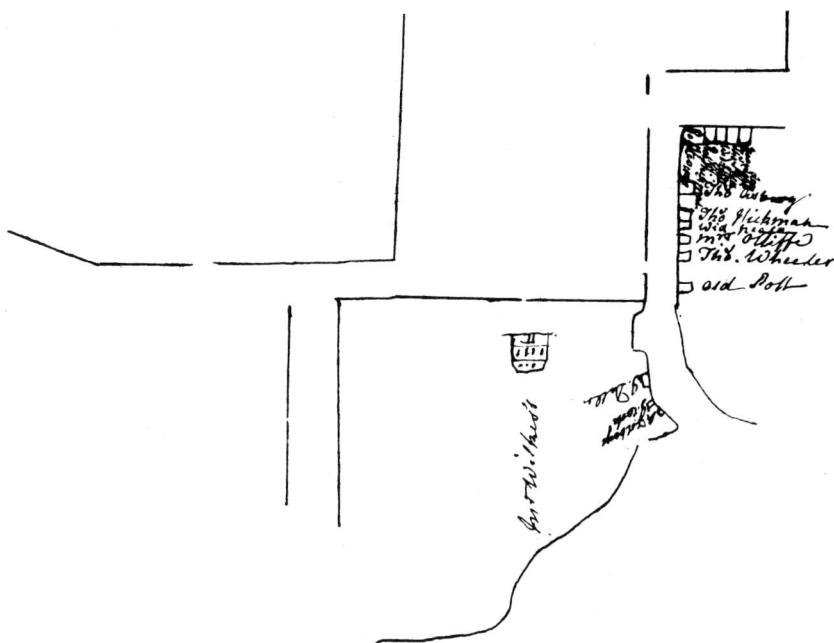

Rough contemporary sketch plan showing occupancy of houses at the corner of Church Street and Parsons Fee, *c.* 1755–60 (p. 42). Also shown is the Prebendal House ("Mr Wilkes"). John Wilkes, the celebrated demagogue, became one of Aylesbury's two M.P.s in 1757.

The implication of this note is, first, that the parish had not been receiving anything from the Charity prior to 1758 and, secondly, that the officers had not insisted on the annual distribution but had contented themselves with payments – probably amounting to no more than a few pounds – sufficient to cover the annual rent of the houses occupied by two poor parishioners.

Robert Hickman, Trustee, 1756–1795

On Joseph's death in 1756 the trusteeship descended to his son Robert Hickman, then aged 30, who seems also to have inherited the Walton Street house. Nothing more is heard of any co-trustees and it is clear that control remained with the family. Robert, though the first child of Joseph to appear in the Aylesbury register, was actually his second son. Thomas, the eldest, birthplace unknown, is said to have lived at least part of his life at Reading and died young there, having married and had a son. He is also said to have been a "pensioner" of Hickman's Charity.[64] Two other children of Joseph's, Ann, born 1730, and William, born 1742, are known to have survived into adulthood. William was living in one of the almshouses by 1780. He became usher, or undermaster, at the Free Grammar School in 1777. The minute recording his election to this office states that the appointment was not on account of any relationship to the founder (i.e. William Phillips) "He having declared in his will that he had no near relations." This has the appearance of a gibe at the notion of founder's kin with which the name of Hickman had come to be so closely associated. Sadly, William died in 1783 at the early age of 41. After his death his sister became an almshouse resident until her death in 1806. Thus between them William and Ann were to occupy an almshouse for perhaps 30 years or so.[65]

A peruquier. Robert Hickman (d. 1795), who at the age of 29 succeeded to the Trusteeship on the death of Joseph Hickman in 1756 (pp. 43–44), was a peruke, or periwig, maker.

Robert himself was a peruke, or periwig, maker, a trade which became obsolescent well before the end of the century. Like his father, Joseph, he kept accounts for the Charity, beginning in 1757, which were likewise deemed on examination

---

64 Lipscomb, *History,* vol. 2, p. 52, pedigree of Hickman of Aylesbury (shows descendants of Robert, the initial trustee, to c.1840 and a few earlier connections inferred from Thomas Hickman's will).

65 BRO Q/RPl/2/1–53, duplicate land tax returns, 1780–1832; CH 3/AM/1, Aylesbury Grammar School minutes, 1720–1816.

by the Commissioners in 1833 to be "imperfect," despite evidence of their having occasionally been audited by the churchwardens. They covered the years from 1757 to 1793, but were found to contain "scarcely any appropriation of money to charitable purposes." On the other hand, there were some entries of payments to his mother and to a brother (Thomas?) in London "in distress."[66] This giving of cash relief to family members was not sanctioned by the founder's will. It is clear, too, that the annual distributions to the poor were completely in abeyance.

66   *The Universal British Directory,* 1792; *26ᵗʰ Report … Concerning Charities,* p. 52.

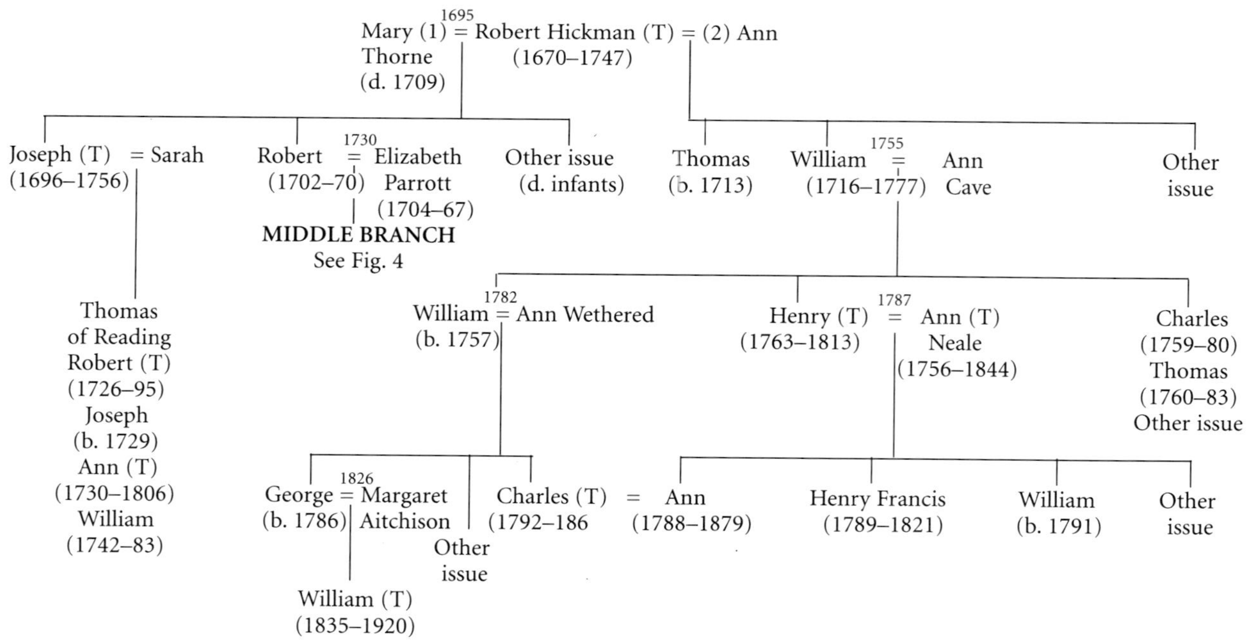

Mary (1) [1695] = Robert Hickman (T) = (2) Ann
Thorne (1670–1747)
(d. 1709)

- Joseph (T) = Sarah (1696–1756)
  - Thomas of Reading
  - Robert (T) (1726–95)
  - Joseph (b. 1729)
  - Ann (T)
  - William (1730–1806)
  - William (1742–83)
- Robert (1702–70) = Elizabeth Parrott (1704–67) [1730]
  MIDDLE BRANCH See Fig. 4
- Other issue (d. infants)
- Thomas (b. 1713)
- William (1716–1777) [1755] = Ann Cave
  - William (b. 1757) [1782] = Ann Wethered
    - George (b. 1786) [1826] = Margaret Aitchison
      - William (T) (1835–1920)
    - Charles (T) (1792–186–) = Ann (1788–1879)
    - Other issue
  - Henry (T) (1763–1813) [1787] = Ann (T) Neale (1756–1844)
    - Henry Francis (1789–1821)
    - William (b. 1791)
    - Other issue
  - Charles (1759–80)
  - Thomas (1760–83)
  - Other issue
- Other issue

Fig. 3 Pedigree showing the descent of the senior and junior branches of the descendants of Robert Hickman (1670–1747)

Note. Figs 3 and 4 are adapted, with amendments and additions, from the more detailed pedigree in G. Lipscomb, *History … of the County of Buckingham*, vol. 2, p. 52; (T) after a name indicates a trustee of Thomas Hickman's Charity.

Plate 1 Cottages "near unto the church gate". The original almshouses as remodelled in 1871. The designs of William White, the architect, are shown on the cover.

Plate 2 Cast plaques similar to the above identify and publicly document the Hickman residences.

Plate 3 This view shows the frontage of the first almshouses onto Parsons Fee. The buildings beyond suggest how they might have looked in Thomas Hickman's day.

Plate 4 These adjoining houses, more recently acquired by the Trust, now provide additional homes for the Hickman residents. Note the variety of architectural styles in this and the view of Church Street opposite.

Plate 5 St Mary's parish church, where the founder was buried, seen from Church Street. The characteristic neo-Tudor chimneys of the almshouses, as rebuilt in 1871, can be seen on the left.

Plate 6 These larger houses further down Church Street retain their late-medieval timber framing behind later facades. Robert Gibbs, the Aylesbury historian, lived for many years in No. 8, then known as Oak Hall, now The Chantry. Today this name embraces the wider complex.

Plate 7 The Hickman residents' bric-a-brac stall in the Chantry gardens, 20 June 1999. They regularly participate in local activities, like this annual "Secret Gardens" event organised by the Aylesbury Old Town Residents Association.

Plate 8 At home in one of the recently converted houses in Castle Street.

5

A Family Affair, 1760–1820

A Family Colony

Meanwhile the middle branch of the family of Robert, the initial trustee, was gradually infiltrating the almshouses. Both the two children of his second son, Robert (1702–1770), were resident by 1780 at the latest. Susannah had married John Asbury in 1757 and John, a carpenter like his father and the last of many successive generations to work in the family trade, had married in 1760. John died in 1790 while Susannah survived until 1824. All three of Susannah's children found places in the almshouses, Sarah (1757–1796), who had married Charles Capell, was resident by 1794 (her husband was still there in 1813), John Asbury, junior (1761–1814), by 1800, and Thomas Asbury (1766–1834) by 1809. They were joined around 1800 by Charlotte (1761–1808), the elder of John's two children – both daughters – and her husband, John Poole (1757–1839), whom she had married in 1788, followed around 1818 by their son William Hickman Poole (1794–1858), a bachelor, and, around 1820, by their daughter Mary Hickman Poole (1790–1831), who had married Henry Reader in 1811. By the following decade Pooles and Readers were beginning to replace Asburys altogether.[67]

The duplicate land tax returns for the period 1780–1832 – the earliest available continuous source of information – at first show only three entries identifiable as almshouses, which may mean that the other two were still occupied by poor parishioners exempted from payment. But by the early 1790s all five almshouses were in the name of a member of the kin. The almshouses were now in fact a kind of family colony and this state of affairs remained the norm rather than the exception for the following half century and more.[68]

---

67 BRO Q/RPl/2/1–53, land tax returns, 1780–1832; Hickman pedigree, printed in Lipscomb's *History,* vol. 2, p. 52. This pedigree is the main source of information about the Asbury-Poole-Reader connection. See Fig. 4.

68 BRO Q/RPl/2/1–53. It should be noted that the land tax returns may not show sub-tenants and lodgers.

The land tax returns also show that the tenant of No.1 Church Street in 1780 was Widow Williams and that Ann Jemmett, doubtless a relation of Robert Jemmett, the trustee, was now occupying No. 11 Market Square.

The relative poverty and the increasing numbers of the middle branch of the family obviously contributed to the changed situation, but the worsening economic climate after 1790, the result of over-population, unemployment and the effects of the French wars, must also have made free housing an ever more desirable commodity. Few houses were being built for the poor and those that were run up were often miserable hovels crowded into narrow courts and inn yards. It is perhaps not surprising that from the 1790s babies were being christened with the middle name Hickman as a reminder of their birthright. The post-war recession after 1815 and the collapse of the local lace trade in the early 1820s in the face of machine-made varieties made matters even worse and sustained improvement in the condition of the poor in southern England did not arrive until after 1845.

Life in the almshouses in the opening decades of the nineteenth century can hardly have been peaceful. Children were born and brought up there and the noise and the overcrowding must at times have been overwhelming. Nor was there any lack of distractions. The church opposite was an endless source of entertainment with its bells and bell ringers, its Sunday services, christenings, marriages and funerals. It was in the church, too, that the town fire engine, manned by volunteer firemen, was kept.[69]

The churchyard also presented a scene of constant animation, for it was here that the Grammar School boys in their quaint uniforms disported themselves, as – after 1810 – did the pupils of the boarding school for young ladies established in the row of cottages next door to the almshouses in Parsons Fee by the youthful Miss Turner. The paupers from the parish workhouse on the corner of Pebble Lane, too, must have been much in evidence. Soldiers from the many regiments billeted in the town are said to have been flogged here. At election times the candidates were, by ancient custom, formally nominated here amid scenes of enthusiasm. Here too during the war years members of the exiled French court from Hartwell House and from nearby Brook Cottage on the Oxford Road could often be seen coming and going. On one memorable day in the April of 1814 the newly-restored French king, Louis XVIII, came by to take his leave of Miss Turner's young ladies, each of whom also received a parting kiss from the king's brother, the Comte D'Artois, afterwards Charles X. One wonders what the Asburys and their relations made of this event.[70]

69 Gibbs, *Aylesbury*, p. 397.
70 *Ibid*, pp. 53, 433; Hugh Hanley, *The Prebendal, Aylesbury. A History* (Aylesbury, 1986), p. 47.

Engraving of St Mary's parish church and churchyard prior to the restoration of the church in 1848–69 showing a funeral in progress.

The Junior Branch Takes on the Trusteeship

When Robert Hickman died unmarried in 1795 his sister Ann, the last surviving member of the senior branch of the family, became the nominal trustee. Whether Ann, then aged 65, actually took any active part in the affairs of the Charity may be doubted, especially as she was illiterate and thus unable to keep the accounts herself.[71] There was also the question of the succession, for since she was the last of the senior branch, it was by no means certain who should inherit the trusteeship.

---

71 *26th Report… Concerning Charities*, p. 52.

As it happened, a possible successor had appeared on the scene in recent years in the person of Henry Hickman, surgeon, apothecary and man midwife.[72] Born in 1763, Henry belonged to the junior branch of the family and was in fact the youngest child of William Hickman, youngest son of Robert, the initial trustee. William had remained a bachelor until the age of 38. Then in 1755 he had married Ann Cave, sixteen years his junior. According to the marriage licence both William and his bride were resident in Aylesbury, but Ann is said to have been the heiress of a Northamptonshire family.[73] If so, we shall probably never know the circumstances behind their secret marriage. Interestingly, in the licence application William describes himself not – as he is elsewhere styled – a carpenter but a turner, a branch of carpentry concerned with the shaping of wood on a lathe and associated more with the making of furniture and small objects than with the building trade.

Doubtless William's marriage improved his status in the community. Certainly two years later his signature appears among those approving the churchwardens' accounts in 1757. Nevertheless he continued to pursue his trade as before, for the same accounts show successive payments totalling over £18 to "Mr William Hickman" for unspecified services to the parish.[74]

William Hickman was evidently something of a radical in politics. When the town's former M.P. was triumphantly returned for Middlesex in 1768 to the cry of "Wilkes and Liberty" in defiance of parliament's authority, William was one of 34 independent-minded Aylesbury electors who petitioned in his support. Such loyalty was the more remarkable in that Wilkes, after he had been forced to flee abroad to escape his creditors in December 1763, was found to have falsified the accounts of the Aylesbury branch of the London Foundling Hospital and among the many local tradesmen left unpaid was William's brother Robert, who was owed over £22.[75] In 1773 William was a subscriber to the new peal of bells in the parish church of St Mary's.[76] He died intestate and a widower in 1777 while staying at Bathford, near Bath in Somerset, perhaps in order to take the spa waters.[77]

---

72 *Universal British Directory.*
73 BRO D/A/M, marriage licence papers; Lipscomb, *History,* vol. 2, p. 52. Stanford-Dingley, the alleged family seat, is actually in Berkshire.
74 BRO PR 11/5/1.
75 Gibbs, *Aylesbury,* p. 232; V. E. Lloyd-Hart, *John Wilkes and the Foundling Hospital at Aylesbury 1759–1768* (Aylesbury, 1979), p. 74.
76 Gibbs, *Aylesbury,* p.27.
77 R. A. Kidd, "Buckinghamshire Wills and Administrations in the Prerogative Court of Canterbury 1700–1800" (typescript index in BRO), p.97.

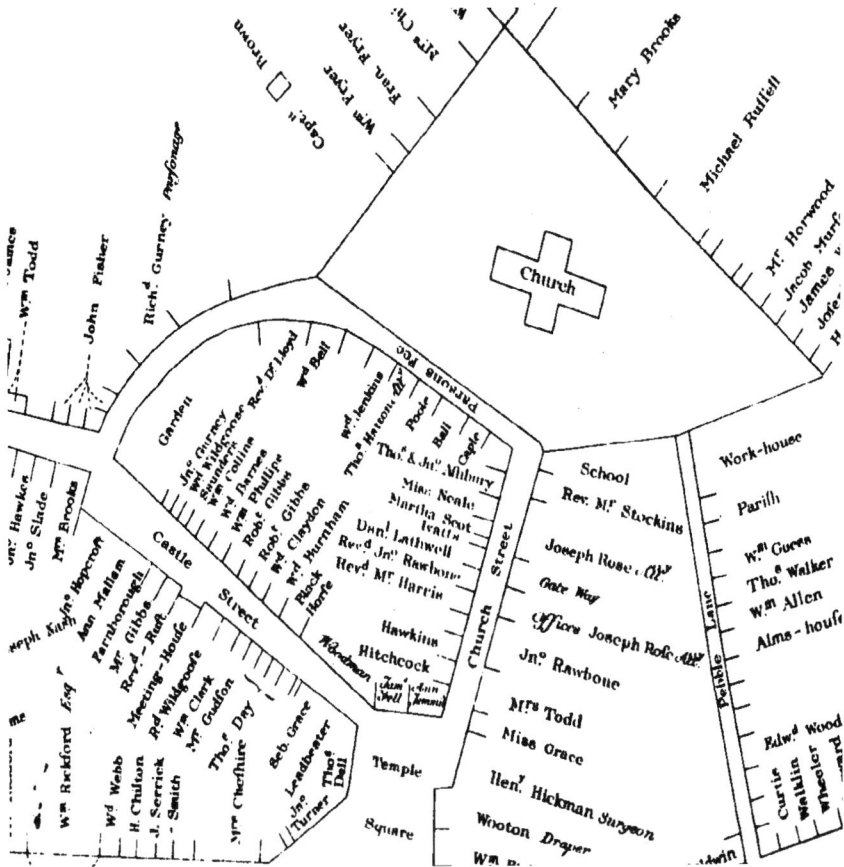

Extract from *A Sketch or Eye-Draught of Aylesbury ...*, by William Rutt, 1809, showing the vicinity of the churchyard. Included are the original 5 almshouses on the corner of Church Street & Parsons Fee, occupied by families of Pooles, Caples (Capell) and Thomas & John Asbury among Hickman kin. Henry Hickman surgeon is shown occupying No 1 Church St, the founder's former residence, at the junction of Church Street & Temple Square.

William and Ann had four sons, two of whom died young and unmarried, and two daughters, all born between 1756 and 1763. Both surviving sons became surgeons, a profession that was rising in the social scale in this period, and the daughters made advantageous marriages.[78] In 1782 William, the elder son, married Ann, only daughter of George Wethered, founder of the well-

78 Lipscomb, *History,* vol. 2, p.52.

Stockins Rev. Wm. A. M. (F.) *Vicar
of Stone*
          PHYSIC.
Hayward William, (F.) *Surgeon, Apo-
thecary, and Man-Midwife*
Hickman Henry, *Surgeon, Apothecary,
and Man-Midwife*
Kenedy Dr. Peter, (F.) *Phyſician*
Wall Wm. (F.) *Chymiſt & Druggiſt*
Wattſon John, *Surgeon and Apothecary*
          LAW.
Adams Edward, *Attorney*
Bull Farmore, (F.) *Attorney*
Burnham Joſeph, (F.) *Attorney*
Chaplin Acton, (F.) *Attorney*
Hatten Thomas, *Attorney*
Parker John, (F.) *Attorney*
Pricitt Benjamin Houghton, *Attorney*
          TRADERS, &c.
Abel Thomas, *Sadler*
Acomb John, *Taylor*
Ames George, *Cordwainer*
Adnum James, *Copperſmith and Warm-
ingpan-maker*
Allen Michael, (F.) *Victualler.*
                    Anſler

Extract from the Aylesbury section of a trade directory, 1792, showing the entry for Henry
Hickman among the physicians.

known Marlow firm of brewers, who had died the previous year, and settled in
Marlow.[79] No member of the bride's family signed the marriage register. Henry,
the younger son, who had been left an orphan at fourteen, married Ann Neale,
daughter of a prosperous family of Aylesbury tradespeople, in 1787; she was
some seven years his senior. After their marriage the couple set up house in No.
1 Church Street, whose previous occupant, Mary Williams, died the same year,
having survived her husband, the apothecary, by nearly thirty years. In the
Aylesbury section of the *Universal British Directory* for 1792 Henry is described
as "Surgeon, Apothecary and Man-Midwife", a combination which by this date

79 *Ibid;* photocopy of Marlow marriage register in BRO.

had become normal as the equivalent of what we would now describe as a general practitioner. The same directory lists two other surgeons-cum-apothecaries (including another man-midwife), in addition to a physician and a "Chymist & Druggist".

The upshot was that, two months before her death in September 1806, Ann Hickman, the trustee, made a brief will leaving all her real and personal property to her "good friend and relation", Mr Henry Hickman of Aylesbury, surgeon and apothecary, and appointing him her executor and that on the strength of this will Henry claimed the trusteeship.[80] His trusteeship was a short one for he died in 1813 at the age of 50.[81]

Although better educated than Ann, Henry, too, failed to keep accounts. After his death some "very imperfect" vouchers and receipts, beginning in

Male doctor examining a female patient, 1822. Henry Hickman, surgeon, apothecary and man-midwife, set up house in No. 1 Church Street, the founder's old house, around 1787 (p. 52) and he became Trustee in 1806 on the death of Ann Hickman.

1806, were produced, but although his widow claimed that he had applied the trust income to charitable purposes, these proved only that he had made regular annual payments of £3 to "the distressed Asburys." The earliest of these payments were in the form "To Asbury as distressed poor," an obvious attempt to bring them within the scope of the distribution provided for in the founder's will; most of the income was unaccounted for.[82]

By his will, made in 1807, Henry left all the property to which he was entitled "either as trustee of Hickman's Charity or otherwise howsoever" to his wife. Ann, who continued to live at No. 1 Church Street, and who also neglected to keep any accounts until 1821, when for the first time a regular charity account book, unfortunately since lost, began to be kept.[83]

80 BRO MS Wills Pec. 7/11.
81 Gibbs, *Aylesbury*, p.35.
82 *26th Report ... Concerning Charities*, p.52.
83 BRO MS Wills Pec. 7/31.

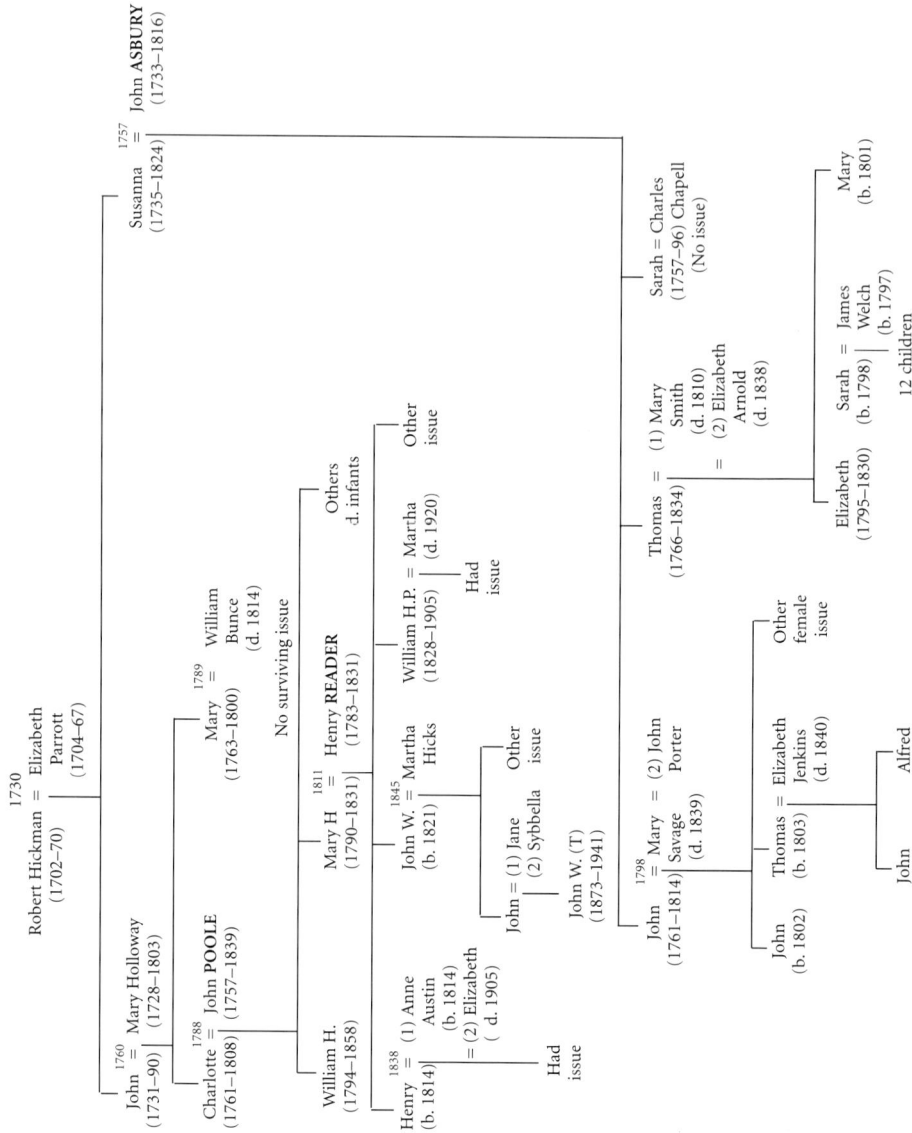

Fig. 4 Pedigree Showing Descent of the Middle Branch of the Descendants of Robert Hickman (1670–1747). See also Fig. 3.

6

Opening Up: Change and Renewal, 1820–1847

The Churchwardens Take an Interest, 1821

It was, it seems, the intervention of the churchwardens which was responsible for the decision to keep accounts. Up to that time Ann had continued to act without their co-operation or interference, but in 1821 an agreement was reached whereby she undertook to allow them to assist in the annual distribution in return for the churchwardens' sanction for her continuing to occupy No. 1 Church Street at a rent of £20 a year, which they considered to be half its true value. The timing of the arrangement may have had something to do with the death in July 1821 of Ann's elder son, Henry Francis Hickman, at the early age of 31. Henry Francis had followed his father's profession and for several years prior to his death had been occupying No. 11 Market Square, where in March 1821 he had been joined in partnership by Robert Ceely, then just embarking upon the distinguished medical career for which he is still remembered in Aylesbury. One imagines that it was young Henry Francis's scientific zeal which was responsible for the inclusion of a post-mortem report on his sister Sarah, who died in 1819, on the family memorial tablet in the parish church. We are told that she was "Suffocated by an abscess of the liver, bursting into the chest, while asleep".[84]

Whatever the circumstances behind the 1821 agreement, it was an important development as it ensured at long last and in a practical way that a proportion of the Charity's income would henceforth be regularly used to benefit the wider population of Aylesbury in accordance with the founder's intentions. It thus provided unambiguous justification for the Charity's status as a public benefaction.

84 Gibbs, *Aylesbury,* pp. 35, 638; Q/RPl/2/39–46.

The 1833 Report

Such justification was needed twelve years later when the Commissioners for Inquiring Concerning Charities visited Aylesbury in 1833, heralding a new era of greater public scrutiny of charities generally. Their published report on Hickman's Charity is the source of the extracts from the early accounts previously cited, as well as of the information about the 1821 agreement.[85]

The Commissioners found that the Charity now consisted of:

1. A dwelling house in Temple Street, "now Broad Street", with a garden, let to Mrs Ann Hickman, the trustee, as yearly tenant, at a rent of £20.

2. A dwelling house in the market place, let by tender to Edward Harrison, as yearly tenant, at a rent of £20. (Pigot's directory for 1830 lists Edward Harrison, Market St, under Chymists and Druggists.)

3. Five "large" cottages near the church gate, occupied as almshouses by the kindred of the testator and another poor person.

4. Four labourers' cottages and about 22 acres of arable land in Walton Field, let to Richard Terry on a 21-year lease from Michaelmas 1822, at a yearly rent of £33. This was considered to be a fair rent, the tenant having laid out £50 to £60 in repairs pursuant to a covenant in the lease.

   (The quantity of land given is too low. The open field land had been consolidated into an allotment of 26 acres under the Walton enclosure award of 1800. The decline in acreage since 1696 is explicable by the use of statute instead of customary acres and by reductions made during the process of enclosure.)

The total income from rents thus amounted to £73 yearly and the total expenditure on land tax, insurance, etc., to £12 12s. 8d., leaving a balance of £60. After payment of all repairs the residue was distributed by the trustee and the churchwardens on New Year's Day (the date of the founder's will).

In referring to one of the occupants of the almshouses as "another poor person," the Commissioners had in mind John Porter, whom they instanced separately as claiming to occupy as one of the kindred, but, they added, "as his only title to that character consists in his having married the widow of John Asbury, one of the kindred, he cannot sustain his occupation as against any of the

85   *26th Report … Concerning Charities,* pp. 50–53.

testator's relations who may be in want of a residence." In the view of the Commissioners he was to be considered as a poor person only and as having a temporary interest. Porter was the second husband of Mary, the widow of John Asbury, junior, who had died in 1814. His case illustrates the difficulties which could arise over the interpretation of "founder's kin." The land tax returns show the other almshouses tenants in 1832 as Thomas Asbury, William Hickman Poole, Henry Reader, and "Asbury and Welsh."

The Commissioners also commented that the almspersons, knowing that all repairs were charged to the Trust, took very little care of their premises, thus causing unnecessary expense. "It is believed that some of them have at times even wantonly damaged their cottages." The cost of these repairs, of course, reduced the amount of the fund available for distribution.

The amount paid to each poor parishioner at the annual distribution is stated to vary between 10s. and £2, given "to poor decayed tradesmen and tradesmen's widows, who have seen better days, and are not in receipt of parish relief. The same objects, with some few exceptions, receive the charity every year." These amounts seem small but at this period many workmen earned no more than a shilling a day. The report added that the poor of Aylesbury receiving parish relief "are of course much dissatisfied with the administration of this charity." The reason for this was that "in this county the receipt of parish alms has become so general, that this class of persons are almost always admitted to partake of the benefit of charities, that are directed by the donors to be distributed only to those persons who receive no parish relief." Reports had even been circulated that the charity "is given to several persons in affluent circumstances." These allegations were, however, rebutted and the Commissioners expressed their opinion that "this charity is productive of great good, and that income is bestowed upon a very deserving class of object, viz. those who are striving earnestly, though with diminished means, to support themselves by honest industry."

The Commissioners refrained from commenting on the position regarding the trusteeship or making any general recommendations. With regard to the tenancy of No. 1 Church Street, they observed that the trustee was "a lady of very advanced age" (she was 76) and that her son, in believing that the existing rent was as much as the house would fetch, disagreed with the churchwardens. On the whole, therefore, they did not think it expedient to suggest any alteration in the arrangement made in 1821. On the other hand, they stated clearly that Mrs Hickman was not entitled to receive the annual payment of £3 which since the very commencement of the then surviving accounts (i.e. since 1746) had been invariably deducted every year by the single trustee administering the charity, but they thought that under the terms of the Will she might legitimately retain £1, the amount allotted to each of the original trustees.

Ann Hickman remained trustee – or "acting trustee", as she described herself – for another ten years.[86] In 1841 the census shows her living in Church Street, alone except for a maidservant. Her death, aged 87, in January 1844, without having made any formal arrangement for the trusteeship, created a new situation, for there was now no obvious successor resident in the town, her three surviving children all having married and moved away.[87]

The 1847 Re-foundation

At this juncture Ann's son-in-law, Charles Hickman, a successful London surgeon then aged 52, stepped into the breach and took on the administration of the Charity. Born at Marlow in January 1792, Charles was the sixth of the eight sons of William Hickman, elder brother of Ann's late husband Henry, of whom at least three had followed careers in medicine. Having qualified M.R.C.S. in 1812 at the tender age of twenty, he had spent his early years in the medical service of the East India Company and was the author of a published account of an outbreak of cholera in the Indian army in 1817. In 1824 he had married his first cousin Ann, eldest daughter of Henry and Ann. By 1846, now on the E.I.C.'s retired list, he was being described in the *London Medical Directory* as a general practitioner living at Denmark Hill in Camberwell.[88]

As a great-grandson of Robert Hickman, the trustee named in the founder's will, Charles had a good claim to the trusteeship. His father, William, who, surprisingly, was still living, 175 years after the birth of his grandfather in 1670, had an even stronger claim as the eldest surviving male heir, but he relinquished it to his son by a legal instrument of 5 October 1844. Nevertheless, father and son decided to regularise the situation by entering a joint petition in the court of Chancery asking the court to exercise its powers to regulate the administration of the Charity.[89]

Significantly, the first task of the court was to determine whether the trust was

---

86   BRO CH 24/E/5/1,lease, 1842.

87   Microfilms of Aylesbury census returns, 1841–91, are held in the County Reference Library. The memorial tablet in the parish church gives Ann Hickman's age at death as 84 (Gibbs, *Aylesbury*, p.35), but it would appear from the parish register that she was the Ann Neale born in November 1756.

88   Lipscomb, vol. 2, p.52; parish registers; the *London Medical Directory* for 1846.

89   Details of the Chancery proceedings are taken from recitals in the trust deed of 30 July 1847 held at Parrott and Coales.

in fact a public charity within the meaning of the most recent relevant legislation. Having decided it was, the court's next task was to discover the heir of the latest survivor of the original trustees of 1696, who would be entitled to the legal ownership. In attempting to decide this point, the court began with the presumption (which happened to be correct) that Robert Hickman had survived his two co-trustees, on the grounds that subsequent trustees had all borne the surname Hickman. Advertisements were ordered to be placed in the *London Gazette* and in newspapers local to Buckinghamshire giving notice that the representatives of the last surviving trustee should appear within 28 days and prove their pedigree or other title as trustee.

PURSUANT to an Order of the High Court of Chancery made in the matter of " Hickman's Chari y," the REPRESENTATIVE or RE-PRESENTATIVES of he SURVIVOR of ROBERT HICKMAN, late of Aylesbury in the County of Bucks, carpenter; Joseph Clayton. late of Bishopstone in the same County, yeoman; and John Plater the younger, of Haddenham, in the same County, yeoman, respectively, deceased, the Devisees in trust named in the will of Thomas Hickman, formerly of Aylesbury aforesaid, gentleman, and who died many years ago, is or are, peremptorily, within Twenty-eight days, to appear before Richard Richards, Esquire, one of the Masters of the said Court, at his Chambers, in Southampton Buildings, Chancery Lane, London, and give notice of his or their title to the said Master ; and are, within Thirty one days after such appearance or notice, to prove his or their pedigree, or other title, as Trustees of the said will.

Advertisement in the *Bucks Herald* relating to the trusteeship of Thomas Hickman's Charity, 26 December 1846. It followed a petition by William and Charles Hickman to the Court of Chancery aimed at regulating the administration of the Charity (pp. 58–59).

This was duly done and the single responder was William Hickman Poole, who asserted his claim to be a trustee as the heir of Robert Hickman, the original trustee. Poole, who was indeed a direct descendant in the female line, had been an occupant of one of the almshouses since before 1820 and was to remain one for the rest of his life. He was well known locally as a travelling bookseller and stationer and as a strong Liberal in politics, with a reputation for honesty and integrity.[90] He did not, however, succeed in proving his claim to the satisfaction of the court and it was disallowed.

The court then proceeded to hear an application from William and Charles Hickman for the appointment of new trustees. They were supported by William Rickford, the well-known Aylesbury banker. As joint founder of Aylesbury's first bank and Member of Parliament for the town from 1818 to 1841, Rickford was a man of considerable experience and authority who had himself been instrumental in reforming the administration of Bedford's Charity. His views were thus

---

90   Parrott, "No. 1 Church Street". Parrott states that Poole lived at No. 1, but this is not supported by the evidence.

likely to carry weight with the court. The upshot was that Charles Hickman was appointed a trustee on the understanding that he would continue to manage the Charity and would personally attend the annual distributions. The Reverend J.R. Pretyman and Zacharias Daniel Hunt were named as co-trustees. Pretyman had been vicar of Aylesbury since 1842. Hunt, then aged about 38, was Rickford's nephew and his partner in the Aylesbury Old Bank.[91]

The court next approved a Scheme for the future regulation of the Charity. While confirming in general the objects of the Charity as expressed in the founder's will, including the privileges accorded to the founder's kin, the Scheme introduced some rules relating to its practical management and provided sanctions to enable their enforcement. Inmates claiming as kin were now to be required to keep their dwellings in the state of repair usually required of yearly tenants and all inmates were to be "orderly, cleanly and moral in their general conduct and habits", failing which they would be liable to removal by the trustees; inmates who were not kin and who received parish relief were to be removed; and the trustees were also to have power to inspect the almshouses and to enquire into the conduct and habits of the inmates.

Other new regulations were concerned with property and finance. The Charity estate was to be let at rack (i.e. market) rents and for terms of not longer than 21 years. Pensions of 4s. weekly were in future to be paid to each almsperson during residence, but were to be discretionary only in the case of persons admitted as kin. The annual distribution to the poor was to be performed jointly with the churchwardens and overseers of the poor, who were to be under a duty to relieve the most deserving and those disabled by sickness, age, infirmity or accident. One other important change involved the introduction of an ex officio element into the trusteeship. Henceforth the vicar of Aylesbury for the time being was to be a trustee, if willing to serve.

The new Scheme was not created by the court on its own initiative but was embodied in the applicants' petition and had been drawn up by their London solicitors, Messrs Chisholme Hill and Gibson, in consultation with the legal representatives of the Aylesbury parish authorities. This is clear from an annotated copy of the petition now in the parish records which shows, for example, that it was the parish's representatives who inserted the provision for weekly payments to the inmates, an arrangement which had obvious attractions since it relieved the ratepayers of responsibility.[92]

91 Alan Dell, *William Rickford, MP (1768–1854)* (Bucks County Library, 1986), pp. 2, 39–42.
92 BRO PR 11/6/72/10.

Brief details of the Charity property were recorded in the court record, including the fact that four of the five almshouses were then occupied by kin and the other by two poor parishioners of Aylesbury. Finally the new arrangements were confirmed by a formal order dated 16 July 1847 and were given legal effect by a conveyance of 30 July to the newly appointed trustees.[93]

93 Trust deed, 1847, at Parrott and Coales.

7

New Trustees, New Almshouses, 1847–1871

The first working meeting of the new trustees took place in the vestry room of the parish church of St Mary the Virgin in February 1848. This was to remain the usual venue for many years, though some early meetings were held at the Old Bank and from 1867 meetings were often held at the office of Messrs Parrott (now Parrott and Coales), solicitors, the clerks to the trustees, whose appointment, oddly, is not recorded in the minutes. At the first meeting the decision was taken to meet annually in January.[94]

Improvements to No. 1 Church Street

The first problem which the new trustees had to cope with was that of finance. The legal expenses of obtaining the new Scheme amounted to £100, charged on the estate, and No. 1 Church Street was in need of extensive repairs, estimated at over £150. Existing tenancies granted in 1846 and 1842 of No. 11 Market Square and the Walton farm were confirmed, the former to Edward Margesson, tobacconist – it was still a tobacconist's shop a century later – for £20 per annum and the latter to Edward Terry, brewer, at £50, reflecting its increased value. Finding a tenant for the Church Street house proved more difficult, but eventually it was let in 1850 to Edward Robert Baynes, solicitor, on a seven-year repairing lease at £25, the trustees agreeing to pay the first £200 of the cost of the repairs. These were much less advantageous terms than had been anticipated: to meet the expenses, and doubtless to avoid having to discontinue the distributions to the poor, a loan of £250 at interest of 4% per annum was requested and obtained from the Old

---

94   Minute book/account book of the trustees, 1847–69, held at Parrott and Coales. Later minute books are also held there with the exception of the minute/account book for 1870–1927, which is in BRO (CH 24/AM/1). Unless otherwise indicated, the minutes are now the source for the text.

The Bourbon Street office of Parrott and Coales (formerly Parrott), Solicitors, clerks to the Charity since 1848 (p. 62).

Bank; it remained a charge on the estate for many years. Hunt's trusteeship must have seemed advantageous to the bank, and was so considered by himself, an example of the exercise of a mild form of patronage.

E. R. Baynes (1816–1898), who is credited in 1860 with having carried out further improvements to the value of £180, for which allowance was again made in the rent, was tenant of the Church Street house for over twenty-five years. He was afterwards Clerk of the Peace for Buckinghamshire from 1880 to 1888. It is he who must have been responsible for the additional short extension to the rear, or garden side, of the house incorporating a ground-floor bay window and a decorative barge board. It is shown on a the town map of 1878 and earlier (minus the bay window) in the 1863 estate map-survey book. The extension made possible the creation of the spacious rectangular dining-room – now used as a meeting room – which with its inserted dark oak antique panelling is the house's most striking interior feature.[95]

The Rebuilding of the Almshouses

In 1862 the trustees turned their attention to the need for landlord's repairs to the almshouses themselves. Estimates were obtained and the two resident trustees, Archdeacon Bickersteth – the energetic new vicar, who had replaced Pretyman as trustee in 1855 – and Z.D. Hunt, were asked to superintend the work. The following year the trustees found it advisable to approach the new Charity Commissioners to urge upon them their desire to put the almshouses "in a state fit for decent habitation" and specifically to convert two of the smaller houses in Parson's Fee into one tenement. First appointed in 1853 to administer most of the powers previously exercised by the court of Chancery, the Charity Commissioners were henceforth to play an important role in the affairs of local charities.

Meanwhile a survey of all the Charity properties was ordered and the resulting volume, containing plans and written particulars of the estate by Frederick Gotto, surveyor, was approved in 1863, when Archdeacon Bickersteth was asked to approach the Commissioners once again on the matter of the repairs.

In January 1864 Bickersteth submitted his correspondence with the Commissioners. It included references to a new Scheme which the Commissioners proposed for the Charity at this juncture, presumably as a preliminary to repairs. This Scheme, details of which are not given in the minutes, the trustees considered to be "unnecessary and inconvenient." But they evidently felt that the existing

---

95 E. Stephens, *The Clerks of the Counties 1360–1960* (1961), p.59; O. S. 1/500 scale map of Aylesbury, surveyed in 1878, in County Reference Library; map-survey book of Charity properties, 1863, held at Parrott and Coales.

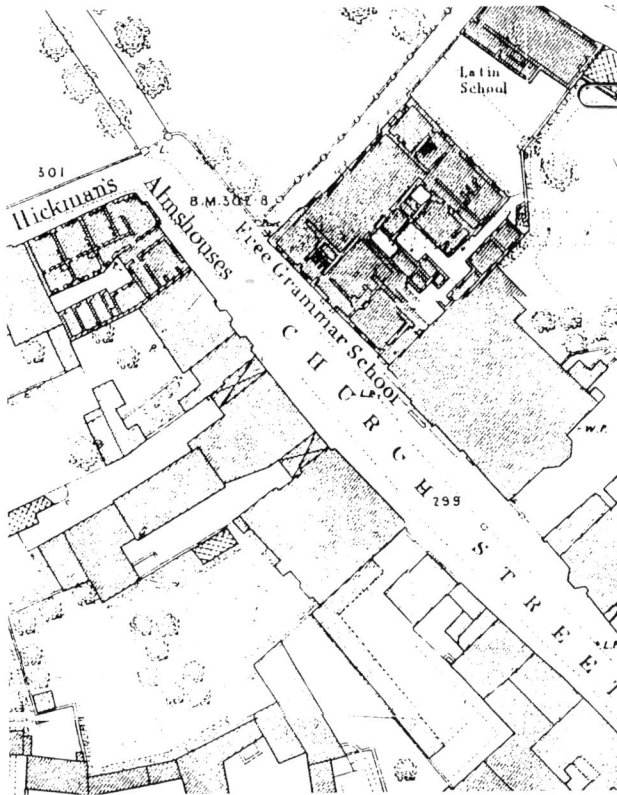

Extract from O.S. 1/500 scale map of Aylesbury showing ground plan of the recently-restored almshouses, 1878. Also shown are the adjoining properties since acquired by the Charity.

Scheme could be improved, for they expressed in rather vague terms a desire for "the admissions to the almshouses to be placed under due regulation to ensure their occupation by poor settled inhabitants of the parish…with a close regard to any such of the same as may be shown to be of kin to the Founder." Clearly the trustees felt that the right of admission ought to be confined to persons who were both local and poor, whether kin or not, a change which would have been contrary to the founder's express intentions to admit "kindred though never so farr of". The trustees also reiterated their wish to put the almshouses into a proper state of repair, revealing that two of them had been "for some time uninhabited owing to their state of decay and defective sanitary arrangements".

The Commissioners, whose remit was to ensure that as far as possible the wishes of donors were observed, were obviously unable to comply with the views of the trustees about admittance to the almshouses, for an alternative Scheme proposed by the trustees in 1866 was rejected, but permission was forthcoming for the rebuilding of the three smaller almshouses situated wholly in Parsons Fee at a cost not exceeding £500.[96]

The estimate for rebuilding the almshouses is dated July 1865 and comes to £455. The architect's plan tracings (see cover illustration) attached to it show that they were originally intended to have bay windows on both floors with window seats inside, but these were omitted, apparently on grounds of economy, a saving of £10. The final cost, including various extras, was approximately £475.[97] The architect was William White, F.S.A., of Wimpole Street, London, and the builder William Green of Aylesbury. The work was completed in April 1867, when it was decided to raise a mortgage of up to £500 to pay for it; in the event, at the insistence of the Charity Commissioners, repayment was by means of another bank loan upon security of the property.

Early in 1871 restoration of the two almshouses in Church Street was proposed and Bickersteth and Hunt again undertook to see what arrangements could be made at a cost not exceeding £400. Nothing more is said about the project in the minutes, but the accounts record cash payments totalling just over £190 in 1871 and 1872 to Thomas Haddon, builder, "for altering and repairing almshouses". The work must have been fairly speedily executed for a tablet on No. 1 Parsons Fee records that "These five cottages ... were repaired and made uniform A.D.1871" and gives the names of the trustees responsible, Zacharias D. Hunt, Edward Bickersteth, D.D., and William Hickman, M.A.

William White (1825–1900), one of the leading architects of the mid-Victorian Gothic school, was involved in many building projects in Buckinghamshire in this period, specialising mainly in church restoration and, to a lesser extent, in schools and vicarages. Surviving examples of his work in the immediate vicinity of Aylesbury include schools at Oving and Cuddington (since altered) and the Elizabethan-style former vicarage at Waddesdon. His writings show that he held advanced views on social housing and favoured subsidised dwellings for the very poor.[98]

The material used in the restoration was red brick and the style has been variously

---

96 An amended version of the existing Scheme was in fact issued by the Commissioners and was dated 11 April 1865. A copy is held at Parrott and Coales.

97 BRO CH24/E/2/2, E/2/4–13.

98 Nickolaus Pevsner and Elizabeth Williamson, *The Buildings of England: Buckinghamshire* (2nd ed.,1994); Paul Thompson, "The Writings of William White", in John Summerson (ed.), *Concerning Architecture....*(1968).

described as a "rather advanced Old English picturesque" and "heavy and ugly Victorian Gothic".[99] With their distinctive round-arched gothic doorways and tall chimneys, the buildings add an unmistakably Victorian touch otherwise largely absent from the varied architecture of the churchyard area. But whatever the verdict on the style and its effects on the streetscape, the rebuilding undeniably gave the almshouses a more institutional appearance and one more calculated to encourage conformity and respectability, an outcome that may not have pleased all the residents.

Although the external appearance of the almshouses was transformed, much of the original medieval timber-framing, including an early cruck structure in the south wall, remains intact behind the brick facade. Comparison with the 1863 map survey indicates that a small, irregular area of yard was incorporated into No. 2 and No. 3 Parsons Fee to provide some additional living space at the rear. The architect's plans show that the Parsons Fee houses each had a living room, a "scullery" and a tiny pantry at the back from which a staircase led up to an upper floor with two bedrooms above, the front one approached by a short corridor. Fitted dressers were supplied, as were sinks and small (2ft 6ins) ranges, with ovens, for cooking. Other amenities included window boards for ironing, forming shutters. On the other hand, as the Charity Commissioners pointed out, there was provision for only one outside "convenience" to serve all the inmates.

The same minutes which report the completion of the first phase of the restoration also note the death on 21 November 1866 of "the late much respected Senior Trustee and the Refounder of this Charity" Charles Hickman. He left personal estate valued at "under £14,000" to his widow, Ann, who died in 1879. In his place was elected his nephew, the Reverend William Hickman, vicar of Christ Church, Warminster, Wiltshire, who was the son of Dr George Hickman, G.P., of Marlow, and was then aged 32.[100]

The Almspeople: Founder's Kin and Others

Although the minutes make only occasional references to the occupants of the almshouses – usually on their admission, but not always then – it is clear that founder's kin continued to dominate in this period. In 1851 the census return indicates that the corner house, No. 1 Parsons Fee, was occupied by James Welsh, aged 52, a labourer at the gas works, his wife, Sarah, a lacemaker, and daughter,

The original almshouses seen from the churchyard opposite, as "repaired and made uniform" in 1871 (p. 66).

Thyrsa H., aged 15, a silk winder, and their "visitors", John H. Trolley, aged 39, a groom, and his wife. Sarah Welsh, born 1798, was the daughter of Thomas Asbury, who had died in 1834. She and her husband had lived in the almshouses since before 1832; they had twelve children, of whom seven were living in 1840. In No. 16 Church Street lived William Hickman Poole, then aged 56, with his house-keeper; and his nephew, William Hickman Poole Reader, a shoemaker, aged 22. The three smaller cottages in Parsons Fee seem to have been occupied respectively by: Henry Reader, a bricklayer, aged 34, his wife, Ann, and their four children, aged 2 to 11; John William Reader, porter and county court bailiff (he later became a successful auctioneer), aged 29, his wife, Martha, and their two children, aged four and two; and Thomas Kempster, a widower, aged 77. Henry and John William Reader were brothers of William H. P. Reader, all three being sons of Henry Reader (died 1831). In all, the occupants of the five cottages numbered nineteen. Thomas Kempster was probably one of the two poor persons of Aylesbury who were mentioned as occupying one of the cottages in 1847.

The proprietary feelings of some of the kindred towards the almshouses is illustrated by an incident which had occurred the previous year when Thomas Kempster was forcibly evicted from his cottage by one of the Readers and was only reinstated when the trustees had recourse to the courts.

In filling the almshouse vacancy created by the death of William Hickman Poole in October 1858 the trustees had to choose between William Hickman Poole Reader, then aged 29, who had been sharing his uncle's cottage, and Mary Hickman White, aged 39, of uncertain pedigree but also claiming as kin. Not only was Mary White's husband, Richard Burt White, not a parishioner but she also had an illegitimate child, born prior to their recent marriage. In the circumstances the clerks to the trustees decided to seek the opinion of the Charity Commissioners as to whether the rule that almspersons should be "orderly, cleanly and moral in their general conduct" could be invoked retrospectively in order to debar her candidature or, failing this, whether "a woman who is of kin and has married a person not qualified either by settlement or kin has … disqual-ified herself and husband from any claims in respect of kin?"[101] The Commissioners' reply cannot have been encouraging for the trustees unani-mously decided in favour of Mary White, her husband being permitted to reside also during her lifetime only. In the event Mary White survived her husband and remained an occupant of the almshouses until her death in 1892.

The following month, November 1858, William Hickman Poole Reader, who by this time had a wife, Martha, and two children, was admitted to the vacancy

THE
"THOMAS HICKMAN ALMSHOUSES."

These Almshouses are intended for Poor Persons who, from Age, Ill-health, Accident, or Infirmity, are unable to maintain themselves by their own exertions. Such Persons having a legal settlement in Aylesbury Parish, and having resided in Aylesbury for not less than three years next preceding their appointment, and being of good character, and regular attendants of Public Worship, are eligible to the Almshouses.

THE FOLLOWING RULES
MUST BE STRICTLY OBSERVED BY THE INMATES:

I.   They are to keep their Houses, with the Offices belonging to them, neat and clean at all times; and in decent repair.

II.   They are not to take Lodgers under any pretence whatever, nor to admit any others to dwell with them, without the permission of the Trustees.

III.   They are to conduct themselves in a quiet and orderly manner, especially endeavouring to maintain peace and charity with their Neighbours.

IV.   They are expected to attend Divine Service regularly.

V.   As the Almshouses are only held on good behaviour, the Trustees will feel it to be their duty to remove any Occupant who shall transgress these Rules.

Aylesbury, May 13, 1867.

Printed *Rules* for the almshouses, 1867 (p. 71).

caused by the death of Thomas Kempster. He, too, was to have a lifelong connection with the almshouses, but on this occasion his stay was a comparatively short one for by 1863 two of the almshouses were empty pending rebuilding and the other three were occupied by Henry Reader (No. 16 Church Street), James Welsh (No. 1 Parsons Fee) and the Whites (No. 4 Parsons Fee).[102]

In 1865 John Reader was paid £5 compensation for fixtures on having vacated one of the Parsons Fee almshouses in 1863 and in 1868, following completion of the first stage of the restoration, the sum of £5, stated to be part of the distribution money, was given to his brother William "who had given up possession of one of the old almshouses." It was also agreed on the latter occasion to seek the sanction of the Charity Commissioners for allowing William 2s. a week from time to time at the discretion of the trustees. Although nothing is explicitly said in the minutes, there must be a suspicion that the trustees were bending the rules – which made no provision for "outdoor" relief to kin – to persuade the brothers, both of whom had young children, not to press their claims to the smaller cottages. The accounts show that William continued to receive an annual pension while a non-resident.

Already in 1867 two special meetings had been held jointly with the parish officers to choose tenants for the two vacancies in the restored almshouses and two poor parishioners, Mary Hearn, a widow, and Elizabeth Piggott were elected; Mary Hearn died the following year and was replaced by Ann Elizabeth Harrison, a retired dressmaker, then aged around 55. The novel experience of appointing poor parishioners as inmates prompted the printing of copies of an outsize notice advertising the charity. In addition to stating the requirements for eligibility the notice incorporated a set of rules of conduct. Inmates were to keep their houses clean and in decent repair; were "not to take Lodgers under any pretence whatever", nor to admit any other in-dwellers without permission; they were to conduct themselves in a quiet and orderly manner; and were "expected" to attend divine service regularly. This last rule, which, one suspects, may have owed much to the clerical trustee, goes some way beyond the provisions of the 1847 Scheme, hence its less peremptory wording.[103]

How much of this applied to the founder's kin resident in the new almshouses is another question. The Whites were restored to the third Parsons Fee house, while Jane Welsh, widow of James, and Elizabeth Reader, widow of Henry (she was evidently his second wife), retained possession of the two houses bordering on Church Street. The latter is described in the 1871 census as a laundress employing three women and her household comprised her unmarried son and stepson, both

---

102 Map survey book of the Charity estate, 1863, at Parrott and Coales.
103 BRO PR11/25/48.

aged 22, a "visitor", Elizabeth Reader, aged 27, and the visitor's two small daughters. Nevertheless after 1868 the founder's kin were never again completely to monopolise the almshouses, nor for that matter did any more young male heads of households ever again take up residence there. In this sense, too, the rebuilding marked a watershed in the history of the Charity.

The Trustees

In 1873 Z.D. Hunt, the last of the trustees appointed in 1847, resigned his trusteeship; he died in 1874 leaving a relatively small personal estate. He was succeeded by Herbert A. P. Cooper, son of Sir Astley Paston Cooper of Gadebridge, Hertfordshire, and a grandson of William Rickford.[104] He held office until 1890, when he was succeeded in his turn by Thomas Horwood, an Aylesbury solicitor, who according to the Aylesbury directory for 1913–14, held the rank of lieutenant-colonel. In 1875 Archdeacon Bickersteth ceased to be a trustee on leaving Aylesbury to become dean of Lichfield. As well as the rebuilding of the almshouses, his time in Aylesbury had also seen the restoration of the parish church of St Mary's. His place was taken by the Reverend Arthur Thomas Lloyd and thereafter by successive vicars of Aylesbury.

104   Dell, *William Rickford*, p. 42.

8

Striking a Balance: the Family and Others, 1871–1950

Changes to the Walton Estate

The eighty years between 1871 and 1950 were relatively uneventful, with no major changes in the constitution or conduct of the Charity. In 1882 just over an acre of land in Walton was sold to the Metropolitan Railway Company, for which compensation of some £600 was received. Doubtless as a result of this windfall, it was proposed that the trustees should acquire additional almshouses. Writing from the Constitutional Club in January 1885, William Hickman reported on an interview he had had with the secretary to the Charity Commissioners on the subject and asked for the address of the gentleman who had lately sold the five cottages adjoining the existing almshouses (Miss Turner's former school premises) who, he understood, was one of the churchwardens for that year. The secretary had expressed the view that "under altered circumstances" the Commissioners might be disposed to favour the proposal, but when Hickman wrote again in March enclosing the Commissioners' formal reply it was not very encouraging and he thought that the trustees would now have "to consider whether it is advisable to apply for a new Scheme." The opportunity passed, for nothing more is heard of the matter and the proposal is not even recorded in the minutes.[105]

In the following year it was decided to take advantage of the 1882 Allotments Extension Act to let out the 16½ acre field in Walton for allotments. The remainder of the property was leased to Henry Landon, who had previously leased the whole Walton estate in 1879, for £34 per annum.

In 1893 the trustees rejected a proposal from the Charity Commissioners to appropriate part of the Charity's funds towards the endowed (i.e. Church) schools. In 1908, the Commissioners in their turn refused consent to the proposed

105 BRO CH24/E/2/3.

Letter from the Rev. William Hickman (1835–1920), the last trustee to bear the family name, 1885, showing first and last pages (p. 73).

sale of the, now redundant, farm buildings at Walton. Instead the Commissioners offered to consider demolishing the existing buildings at Walton and replacing them with "small villas", but the trustees thought that this would "materially decrease the revenue". Eventually in November 1908 consent was given for the sale of the property to Mr Landon for £500.[106] The sale took place in 1909.

The Almspeople, 1871–1907

Though diminished in number, the founder's kin who still resided in the almshouses continued to be difficult to control on occasion, being in some cases relatively young and able-bodied. Mary White, whose arrival in 1859 had caused such a stir, was informed in 1877 and again in 1880 that her son, who was living

---

106　BRO CH24/AM/1, Charity Commissioners' order of 10 Nov. 1908; the property included three cottages (Nos. 25, 27 and 29 Walton Road).

with her, was "not a fit inmate for the almshouse," but Mrs White knew that in practice there was nothing much the trustees could do about it and it is no surprise to find that her son James, then aged 37 and describing himself as a "Firewood Dealer (wholesale)", was still installed in No. 4 Parsons Fee as late as 1891.

In 1882 it was decided that Elizabeth Reader, at No. 16 Church Street, should be informed that "the Trustees could not pay for the water used by her for the purposes of her business as a laundress." This met with no response and a financial induce-ment in the form of an extra allowance of 2s. weekly if she discontinued taking in washing, offered in 1884, was equally unsuccessful. The following year Mr Hickman, in the letter previously quoted, commented on the Charity's existing Scheme, "There are some irregularities attendant upon it now which might be obviated by a Proper Scheme, such as an Inmate taking washing and keeping people to work at it in the almshouse – a thing I very much object to." But once again, in the 1891 census Mrs Reader, now aged 68, was described as "laundress", and her little thirteen-year-old grandson living with her was described as "errand boy."

A Victorian laundress, by John Vince. Elizabeth Reader, described in the 1871 census as a laundress employing three women, operated her business from one of the almshouses in Church Street. In 1882 the Trustees informed her that they could not pay for the water her business used.

The almspeople not claiming as founder's kin who were appointed after 1868 were virtually all elderly, unmarried or widowed and female and this was to be the pattern in the future also. Vacancies, when they occurred, often attracted six or more applications, an indication of the popularity of the new almshouses. One step which the trustees took in 1878 in the interest of good order was to require future inmates to sign written agreements to conform to the regulations contained in the 1847 Scheme.

By 1891 Mary White and Elizabeth Reader were the only two occupants claim-ing as kin. Mrs White died in 1892 and Mrs Reader in 1905. In the meantime

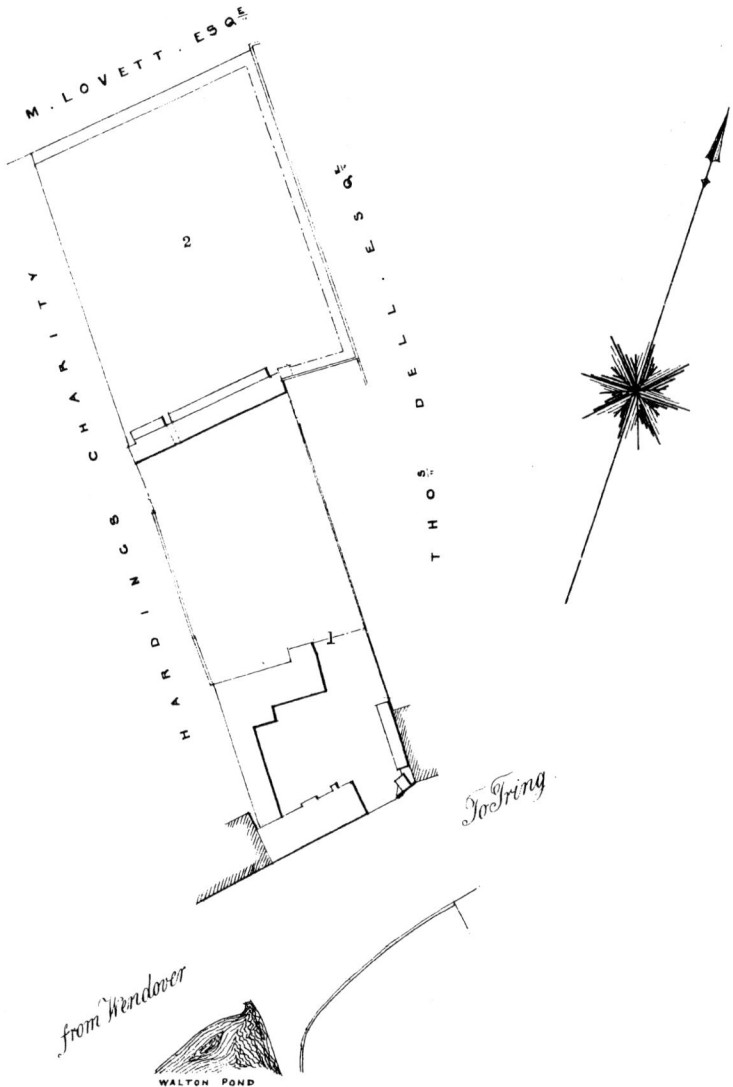

Plan of the former Walton farm premises on the north side of Walton Road in 1863, then described as three cottages, farmstead, rickyard and close. The farm premises (but not the land) were sold in 1909 (p. 74). The site is now occupied by William Harding Close and almshouses. The Walton property was listed by the Commissioners for Inquiring into Charities in 1833 (p. 56).

William Hickman Poole Reader and his wife Martha had been readmitted in 1894, having brought up a family in the interval since their departure in 1863. William died in 1905, but Martha lived on until 1920. The election of Sarah Hickman King and her husband, Joseph John King, in 1905 restored the balance and in 1907 the number of houses occupied by kin rose to three when Mrs Martha Hickman Flitney and Eli W. Flitney moved in.

The Annual Distribution

No annual distribution was made in 1870 on account of the large expenditure in rebuilding the almshouses, but it was resumed in 1871 – when the amount was £32 – and following years. By the 1880s and 1890s the annual amounts varied between just under £40 and £70. In 1909 £51 was distributed in alms and £52 in allowances to inmates, out of a total expenditure of £138. Total income was £166 (more than twice that of 1832), of which £127 was from rents and the rest from dividends on capital invested from the proceeds of the sales in 1882 and 1909. The figures were much the same in 1926 except that expenditure was up on account of an additional £18 spent on repairs.[107]

Tenants and Trustees

Following the departure of E. R. Baynes, No. 1 Church Street had been let in 1879 on a 14-year lease at £45 yearly to Richard Wilson Wilcox, a surgeon who was in partnership with Charles Hooper of Temple Square. In 1888 the lease was assigned to Thomas Godfrey Parrott, Mr Hooper's successor in the partnership. Dr Parrott was still a bachelor in 1891, but he later married Mr Hooper's niece and brought up a family in the house. During his training at King's College Hospital Dr Parrott had worked with Lord Lister, the pioneer of antiseptic surgery. He was medical officer of health for Aylesbury from 1905 to 1938 and remained at No. 1 until his death in 1951.[108] No. 11 Market Square was let to George Margesson Adams, a tobacconist, in 1925 for 14 years on a full repairing lease of £80 a year; in 1887 the tenancy had been offered to Robert Scott, grocer, at £32 a year.

In December 1920 the Reverend William Hickman died after a trusteeship lasting over fifty years leaving a personal estate of £18,000. For some years before his death he had been living in retirement near Maidenhead. As the last of his name

---

107 BRO CH24/FA/2, annual statements of account (4) incorporaring schedules of property and names of inmates, 1909–26.
108 Parrott, "No. 1 Church Street".

to act as a trustee his passing marked the end of an era. His successor was John William Reader, of the well-known Aylesbury firm of auctioneers. Born in 1873, he was the son of John Reader and the grandson of John William Reader, the former court bailiff and Parsons Fee resident. He was thus the first, and only, member of the middle branch of the Aylesbury Hickmans to become a trustee of the charity. He died in 1941.

Founder's Kin, 1920 Onwards

In 1920 the number of houses occupied by founder's kin had again fallen to two and it remained at this level, with one or two short fluctuations, until 1955, when it declined to one, rising briefly to two in 1966. For almost the whole of this period No. 16 Church Street was one of the two. Much less is known about the attributes and family relationships of these tenants than before 1900, but it is clear, for example, that as a group they continued to be younger on admission than the others and that they included males as well as females and at least one married couple. Few seem to have been local to Aylesbury, applications being received from as far afield as Manchester. Surnames were now more diverse. A Mr Frank Reader, who was admitted in 1933, was the only Reader after 1920. The King family were the most dominant branch that can be identified. Sarah Hickman King and her husband, J.J. King, were succeeded by their daughter, Annie Wise, on Mr King's death in 1923. A Kate King was admitted in 1931, having previously applied in 1920, and a Mr George King was elected in 1933, but withdrew to await a vacancy in one of the larger houses. The average period of residence of kin was long. Elizabeth Flitney seems to have been still resident in the 1940s; Annie Wise stayed 16 years; Kate King 19 years; and Frank Reader 22 years.

9

Changing Fortunes: the Post-War Era, 1950–1972

The Pace Quickens

The whole of the period bounded by the two world wars saw no significant changes in the overall position of the Charity, as reflected in the minutes. Towards the end of the 1940s, however, the pace of events abruptly quickened as the trustees found themselves grappling with the problems and opportunities attendant upon Aylesbury's transformation from a quiet market town to a large urban centre. Meetings became more frequent and expert legal and commercial advice became more and more necessary in the face of rapidly rising property values, planning legislation and the fluctuations of the national economy and of government policy. In 1948 No. 11 Market Square was found to be subject to a standard rent of £100 under the terms of the Rent Act. To get around this difficulty the expedient of imposing a premium of £1,000 for the signing of a new lease was adopted. In the following year the first of many offers to purchase this property was firmly resisted. In 1950, when H. Stevens, the new lessees, sought permission to make improvements, the trustees made it clear that, as the building was entirely in keeping with the other ancient buildings fronting the square, they "strongly deprecated any attempt to modernise its external appearance." However, the old shop front, believed to date back to 1775, was found to have become "so perished as to be past repair" and was removed the following year.[109]

In 1954 it was agreed to apply for a change of use of No. 1 Church Street, listed as a building of special architectural or historical interest and now vacant following the death of Dr Parrott, from residential to office accommodation. It was let the following year to Horwood and James, solicitors, for 21 years on a full repairing lease of £200 a year, rising to £300 a year after ten years.

109   Hayward Parrott, *Annals of Aylesbury* (Aylesbury, 1952, booklet), p.52.

Development on the Agenda

In June 1959 the question of the future development of the allotment land at Wendover Road in Walton came on to the agenda when an offer of £30,000 was received for the property. It was rarely to leave it for the next thirteen years. Throughout most of this period the trustees were the Reverend (later Canon) Henry Adeane Bayard, appointed in 1945; Reginald Davey (1948–1968); and Hayward Parrott, who succeeded W.H.E. Gilkes in 1964. A local historian and the author of several published works on Aylesbury, Hayward Parrott, who was a solicitor by profession, was the son of Dr Parrott; he had spent much of his life in No. 1 Church Street and was still living there in 1952.

The allotments directly adjoined Elm Farm, a 52-acre holding belonging to the trustees of Harding's Charity, who were also being pressed by numerous applications to sell. Aylesbury Borough Council wanted to open negotiations for both charity properties. Harding's preferred a public auction in principle, but wished to ascertain the views of the Hickman's trustees before acting. The trustees unanimously agreed that "the time was now ripe" for putting the property on the market and that a sale by public auction was desirable. Accordingly, early in 1960 an application was made for planning permission for residential development. When the application was rejected as premature – the land in question having been scheduled for development in the second phase of the Town Plan, due to begin in 1964 – an appeal was entered. While it was pending the trustees sought to strengthen their position by negotiating the purchase of 1.8 acres of additional adjoining land which would be needed for drainage by any future developer. The Borough Council for its part first offered to purchase the land by private treaty and, when the appeal was dismissed in May 1962, threatened a compulsory purchase order. The trustees' policy was now to seek to retain the land until 1964 for private development as a "good-class residential area."

Demolition of No. 11 Market Square

Meanwhile an unexpected crisis had arisen over No. 11 Market Square, the lease of which had been assigned to R.M. Adams in 1955. In 1960 proposed structural works to the adjoining building had been the subject of an indemnity agreement with the owners, but when the works began in September 1962 No. 11 was found to be in a much worse state than had been realised and the trustees were forced to consent to its demolition as a dangerous structure. Its removal brought into full view again the front of the ancient King's Head inn in all its glory for the first time for centuries. The Borough Council then sought to acquire the site by compulsory

Entrance passage to the fifteenth-century King's Head inn in Market Square. The building on the left (now a travel agency) is part of the Charity's endowment.

purchase but changed its mind. As a further complication the insurers for the adjoining owners repudiated the claim for compensation on the grounds of pre-existing defects and the trustees were forced to take legal proceedings. Finally, the Charity Commissioners refused to sanction the trustees rebuilding on their own account so a 99-year building lease was negotiated with the existing tenants at an initial rent of £620 per annum, with the unimpressive results that can still be seen.

The Sale of the Walton Estate

The years 1964 and 1965 were critical for the future of the Charity. Having decided to submit a new planning application, the trustees reluctantly agreed, on expert advice, to negotiate privately with the Borough Council. The Council offered £5,000 an acre, or £100,000 in total, including the additional land acquired for drainage. Influenced by gloomy prognostications about the effect of then current Labour government policies on future land prices – later to prove unfounded – the trustees sought the consent of the Charity Commissioners to the deal. Consent was refused. In December 1965 the decision was taken to submit fresh planning applications on behalf of both charities.

Then followed extensive consultations with the planning officer and with Harding's to prepare an outline

Old pump in the back yard of the original almshouses, by Rachel Beckett. Doubtless the pump was the source of the water for Elizabeth Reader's laundry, as well as for all the other Hickman residents' needs for drinking and washing until mains water was supplied this century.

development map, in the course of which the trustees were able to make a significant contribution to the detailed planning process, including provision for accommodation for twelve old people. The outcome was the signing of a joint planning agreement on behalf of the two charities and the granting of planning permission in December 1969. The sale of part of the combined site to Sunley Homes for £1,955,000 followed in September 1972.

Plans for Improvements

The prospect of a greatly increased income was the more welcome as the inadequacies of the almshouses buildings were such that they were beginning to prove unacceptable to prospective occupiers. Electricity had only been connected to No. 4 Parsons Fee as recently as 1949 and the outside toilets were without lights until 1968; none of the houses had bathrooms. In 1969 Miss G.M. de Fraine, the occupier of one of the neighbouring cottages in Parsons Fee, wrote to protest at the lack of amenities in the almshouses. In July of the same year it was agreed that all the houses ought to be brought up to modern standards of comfort, with indoor sanitation and bathrooms, and that this could only be done by converting the five into three or four. It was agreed not to re-let the houses as they became vacant in order to expedite conversion when funds should become available. In December 1971 – a century on from the completion of the Victorian rebuilding – plans for conversion, prepared by J.H. Cox Architects Partnership to create three almshouses incorporating inside toilets and suitable kitchens and larders, were approved.

10

New Beginnings, 1972–1998

The Expansion Begins, 1972–73

Although all the land belonging to Hickman's was actually included in the sale of September 1972, the disposal of the Walton property as a whole had been organised as a joint venture with the William Harding Charity in several phases spread over three years and the proceeds were not finally apportioned until 1977, Hickman's share of the capital being just under a million pounds. In the interim the interest accruing was placed in a temporary fund to which both charities had access for their immediate needs. Hickman's annual share of this amounted to more than the total aggregated income received by the Charity during the previous half century.

The transformation in the Charity's circumstances is graphically symbolised by the change in the format of the minutes of the meetings of the trustees. In February 1972 the bald hand-written summary which had sufficed as a record since 1847 is abruptly replaced by a much fuller version, immaculately laid out and expertly typed.

Immediately prior to the sale the trustees had agreed that the modernisation of the existing almshouses would have prior call on the funds and that their second project would be the building of new almshouses on the land which had been purchased for drainage in 1962. This piece of land, comprising 1.8 acres situated at the rear of Eleanor Gardens, had been excepted from the sale and was intended to be the site of ten purpose-built almshouses. Circumstances were to dictate otherwise.

Plans for the modernisation of the existing almshouses had already been drafted and approved. In order for the work to proceed it only remained to find alternative accommodation for the three remaining occupants. But rented accommodation of all kinds was at a premium in Aylesbury in 1972 and all efforts to find something suitable proved vain. This seemingly minor difficulty, which threatened to hold up the conversion scheme, due to begin in March 1973, had important consequences for the future of the Charity estate, for in December 1972 it was agreed to seek the permission of the Charity Commissioners to purchase three suitable houses for temporary use by the tenants and afterwards "for other beneficiaries".

Enquiries to local estate agents were again unproductive, but at a trustees' meeting held in February 1973 Mr Gilkes mentioned that "certain cottages in Castle Street" had recently come on the market. It later transpired that the cottages in question – Nos. 7/15 Castle Street – were a row of five and that they were owned by Castle Properties Ltd, of Castle Street, of which Mr Gilkes was a director; he duly declared an interest. Five cottages were more than was required, but the surveyor's report was enthusiastic on the grounds of the property's "admirable" position, desirability as an investment and the "few if any opportunities … of buying a similar block of houses in the centre of the town". The asking price was £49,250.

The trustees agreed to apply to the Charity Commission for its consent to the purchase on the understanding that the property would be retained for permanent use as almshouses. Meanwhile they decided to seek the views of The National Association of Almshouses on its suitability. The Association's comments were not encouraging, instancing the three floor levels, difficult staircases and the high cost of alterations, but they failed to shake the trustees' resolve not to miss what they saw as a unique opportunity. In May a representative from the Association inspected the cottages in person at the request of the Charity Commissioners and decided that they were, after all, suitable for almshouses and the property was accordingly acquired the following October. The expansion had begun.

Conversion and Extension of Existing Almshouses, 1975–78

Owing to delays caused in part by the need to carry out temporary re-furbishments at Castle Street it was not until December 1974 that the existing almshouses were vacated and conversion work could at last begin, over eighteen months later than planned. The three tenants who moved to Castle Street were Mrs Violet Conway, who had occupied No. 16 Church Street since 1966, Miss Annie Bailey, a tenant since 1951, and Mrs Elicia Adams, who had been admitted in 1954 at the age of 71. Mrs Conway, originally from Blackburn, and Miss Bailey, formerly of Oldham, were both founder's kin.

Frustrating though it must have been, the delay proved fortunate, for in the interval No. 12 Church Street (formerly Nos. 12 and 14), which immediately adjoined No. 16, had come on to the market. The surveyor pointed out that, by demolishing the boundary wall and making the garden of No. 12 available for all the properties, "a vast improvement would result". Since the work had not yet commenced on the existing almshouses, the asking price of £30,000 could be met from accumulated income. It was agreed to proceed and by September 1975 the property had been acquired for £27,000 with planning permission for conversion to four units.

Conversion of the original almshouses, now to be known respectively as No. 16 Church Street and Nos. 1, 2 and 3 Parsons Fee, was completed by the end of 1975 at an estimated cost of £30,000 and the tenants were moved back early the following year. Mrs Adams had died shortly before the move, leaving only Mrs Conway and Miss Bailey to make the short journey from Castle Street. They were joined by Mrs Elsie Waters, aged 76, from Bletchley, and her husband, who had been appointed to the other vacancy on the strength of Mrs Waters's claimed kinship to the founder. Thus all three of the first occupants of the newly converted almshouses were founder's kin.

Conversion of No. 12 Church Street began in October 1976 and was completed in mid 1978 at an estimated cost of £42,000. During the course of the works the original fifteenth-century overhanging first-floor front of the building was found to be intact beneath the later rendering. In consultation with the County Council and the Department of the Environment and with the help of grant aid the decision was taken to expose and restore the close central vertical posts of the timber-framing, leaving rendered in-fill panels between. The outcome was a striking reminder of Aylesbury's concealed heritage of medieval buildings and a more varied and attractive street composition.

New Management Scheme, 1979

The question of a new governing instrument for the Charity to take account of altered circumstances was raised in September 1975 when Mrs H. M. Phillips, solicitor to the Charity Commissioners, attended a meeting of the trustees to discuss the legal formalities required to bring the new property acquisitions within the scope of the existing Scheme. After some discussion about its scope it was agreed to lodge a formal application to the Commissioners for a new Scheme and the resulting draft was agreed by the trustees the following April, subject to certain unstated amendments which they wished to be made. By May 1977 a revised draft was ready for public consultation, but for technical reasons it was not finally sealed until 22 June 1979.[110]

The more important changes effected by the new Scheme may be summarised under three principal headings:

---

110   Charity Commission Scheme for the regulation of Thomas Hickman's Charity, 22 June 1979.

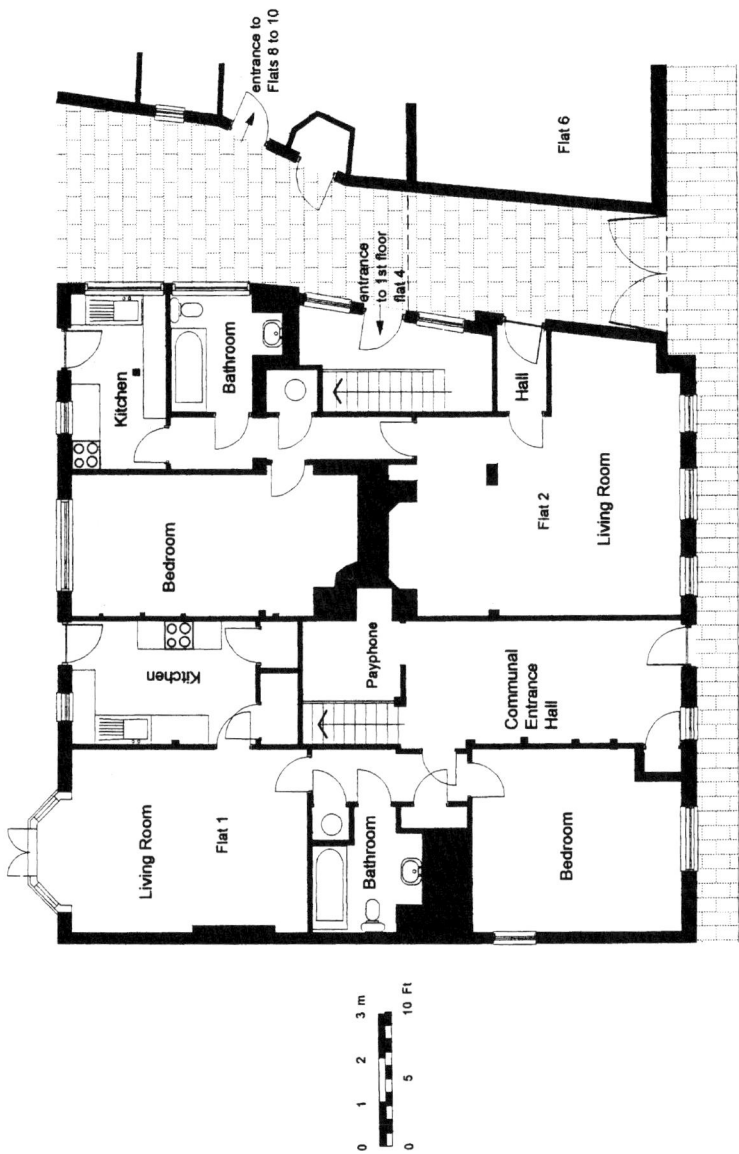

Present ground plan of No. 8 Church Street showing Flats 1 and 2, The Chantry, and entrance passage. Part of the same area is shown in an earlier sketch plan of 1900 (see p. 93).

Trustees
There were in future to be five trustees, which was the minimum number which the Charity Commissioners considered appropriate to the circumstances. They would comprise one ex-officio (the incumbent of St Mary's, Aylesbury) and four co-optative trustees. The latter were to serve for five years only, but could be re-appointed.

Almshouses and Almspeople
As previously, poor persons resident in Aylesbury were to be eligible, but a minimum of three years residence was now stipulated. Founder's kin were to continue to be given preference and need not be Aylesbury residents, but for the first time such preference was made conditional on need. Significantly, too, a person appointed under this heading would in future be required to sign a declaration that he or she did not claim to occupy in his or her own right. Clearly the notion of legal entitlement was being laid to rest.

The weekly stipend to residents established in 1847 and still being paid at the rate of 40p in 1979 was omitted from the new Scheme and instead the trustees were authorised to require occupants to contribute to the cost of maintaining the almshouses.

Relief in Need
Under this heading the trustees were given extensive powers "to relieve either generally or individually persons resident in Aylesbury who are in conditions of need, hardship or distress". The annual distribution was not specified as such.

The co-optative trustees named in the Scheme were Hayward Parrott and L. H. E. Gilkes, existing trustees, W. H. Harman and P. F. Ryan, the latter described as a probation officer. The ex-officio trustee, not named, was the Reverend (later Canon) Peter Graham, who had succeeded Canon Byard as vicar of Aylesbury in 1972. Mr Parrott resigned in December 1981 some months short of his seventy-fifth birthday and died the following May.

No More Founder's Kin

After 1979 few enquiries from persons claiming to be founder's kin were received. In 1980 a Mr King, resident in the United States, sent in an application asking for a house and garden, but did not renew it when informed that there were no houses vacant and that none had individual gardens. In 1982 a precedent was set when a female applicant from Manchester was refused on the grounds that she was only in her mid fifties and "the trustees felt that the older residents of Aylesbury were more deserving of consideration".

After this no more such applications are recorded in the minutes. Thus on the death of Miss Bailey in 1986 for the first time since the early eighteenth century there were no founder's kin resident in the almshouses. The privilege remains, however, and is not without its uses, for it was discovered in 1975 that, because it included a category of beneficiaries not subject to a local residence qualification, Hickman's did not come within the definition of a parochial charity and conse-quently that attendance by representatives of the local authority at some of the trustees' meetings could be discontinued.

Expansion in Castle Street, 1978–85

Meanwhile, in January 1979, a few months prior to the sealing of the new Scheme, work had begun on the conversion of the Castle Street cottages to flats at an esti-mated cost of £98,375. No other projects were now pending, with the exception of No. 4 Church Street, a small house which had been purchased for £10,000 in 1977 and was eventually converted into two dwellings in 1980. In March 1980, when the conversion of Nos. 7/15 was nearing completion, it was decided to acquire Unity Hall, No. 17 Castle Street, a former Independent chapel, latterly used as a club, for £27,500 with planning permission to demolish and to erect seven purpose-built bed-sitting-room flats on the site. Construction work on the new flats was sched-uled to begin in August 1981 at an estimated cost of £128,000 and was completed in December 1982.

During all this time the fate of the site at Eleanor Gardens, which the trustees had been on the point of selling in 1975, when it was feared that it might incur development tax, remained in abeyance. In April 1981 it was again considered and rejected – this time finally – as being "too far from town and not near any shops". It was eventually sold for £109,000 in January 1982.

By January 1984 the number of properties and tenants had increased to the point that it was found advisable to enter into a management agreement with James Cox and Associates, the architects, covering all aspects of maintenance, including – to the considerable relief of the trustees – routine requests and complaints from the tenants. General administrative, legal and secretarial services continued to be supplied by Parrott and Coales.

The years 1983 to 1985 proved to be critical in the evolution of the Charity estate. Further purchases were made in upper Castle Street, this time on the oppo-site side of the street. No. 14 Castle Street was purchased in December 1983 for

£35,500, No. 10 in January 1984 for £24,000 and No. 22 in January 1985 for £35,500, but no conversion work was undertaken for the time being.

The Quest for a Greenfield Site, 1984–85

While continuing to acquire older houses for conversion the trustees were also on the look out for a greenfield site to replace Eleanor Gardens, but none of those looked at proved acceptable. In January 1984 the minutes record that they were "disappointed that they had been unable to procure a suitable block of land for development as almshouses". This renewed interest seems to have been inspired in part by the growing realisation of the need for forward planning to provide a better mix of accommodation which should include double units for married couples. Bed-sits, it was agreed, should in future be avoided if possible as "it was obvious that occupants preferred separate bed and sitting rooms".

In reality a suitable development site had already been found by January 1984 but the negotiations were hanging fire. This was a piece of land belonging to St Mary's School at Mill Way on the ring road which had been offered for sale by the diocesan authorities. Purchase was agreed by February 1985 at £57,500 and the architects were asked to prepare plans for four self-contained flats with separate entrances, it being "of paramount importance that residents should be free of the difficulties which communal entrances and staircases were likely to engender".

An Opportunity in Church Street, 1984

But while this transaction was still in train attention had once again switched to Church Street where the freehold of No. 10, a substantial property adjoining the existing Parsons Fee complex, came on the market in April 1984. Taking into account the high cost of conversion, the surveyors were unable to recommend purchase at the asking price of £200,000, but during the discussion it emerged that the adjoining property, No. 8, known as The Chantry, was also likely to come on the market before long and it was realised that:

> "If that property could be acquired as well, then a much more compre-hensive development could take place, incorporating the large garden of No. 8 and part of the garden of No.14 Castle Street, which the trustees already owned."

This was the germ of the self-contained almshouse development now known collectively as The Chantry.

As it turned out, an offer of £165,000 for No. 10 without prior planning permission was accepted and the conveyance was executed by June 1985. The

Above. No. 8 Church Street showing the main carriage entrance to the Chantry complex. Below. View of the interior courtyard taken from an upstairs flat showing the bungalow units erected in 1989–90. The roofs of adjoining older houses in Castle Street can be seen in the background.

same month No. 8 at last became available and in August the trustees agreed that there was no option but to pay the full asking price of £210,000 since it was now seen as "vital" to their scheme. Planning could now proceed on a comprehensive basis for a site which would include over an acre of open space at the rear.

The Chantry Project, 1984–90

For the following five years The Chantry project was central to the trustees' concerns and it has influenced such additional purchases as have since been made. In November 1986 the architects were ready with their layout plan for eleven converted flats and nine purpose-built bungalow units – more than had been envisaged at Mount Street – on the vacant land behind. "The philosophy behind the scheme", Mr James Cox told the trustees, "was to produce a feeling of total community for the project as a whole, linked to the Charity's existing development in Church Street and Castle Street". The cost of the work was roughly estimated at half a million pounds.

At this late stage some reservations were expressed that the number of new buildings would make the scheme too intensive and might "further accentuate the imbalance in the community with elderly people being congregated near the town centre", but Mr Gilkes pointed out that elderly people had always lived in this particular area of the town and the consensus was in favour of the scheme as it stood.

In embarking on so major a project the trustees were conscious of the difficulties they faced. In the first place there was the problem of costs in relation to liquid assets since any funds taken from the permanent investment endowment would have to be repaid over time. There was also the need to avoid having too many projects in hand at the same time. The first difficulty was surmounted by fortunate timing and good advice, despite the adverse effects of the stock market crash of 1987 on investment income; the second by agreeing, if necessary, to shelve the St Mary's school site development. The latter project had in fact effectively shelved itself, as delays multiplied. By the time that the sale contract was at last ready for signing in July 1987 the trustees were having second thoughts and described themselves as "somewhat unenthusiastic about the transaction" because of inconvenience of location. It was accordingly decided to offer the property to the William Harding's Charity, which was also seeking a site for almshouses and was happy to take over the purchase.

Another difficulty concerned planning permission. Both No. 8 and No. 10 Church Street were important listed buildings needing sensitive handling. Like most of the houses in Church Street, both were late-medieval buildings of timber-framed construction behind later brick facades. No. 10 has a handsome eighteenth-century front in dark brickwork with stucco cornice and window surrounds and a pedimented doorcase. No. 8 (The Chantry), which at one time was the residence of Robert Gibbs, historian of Aylesbury, is triple-gabled with an elaborate stuccoed early nineteenth-century Gothic front complete with decorated barge boards and diamond-glazed windows. Its fine carriage entrance has since become the main entrance to the complex.

Both houses also had important interior features such as fireplaces. It is thus

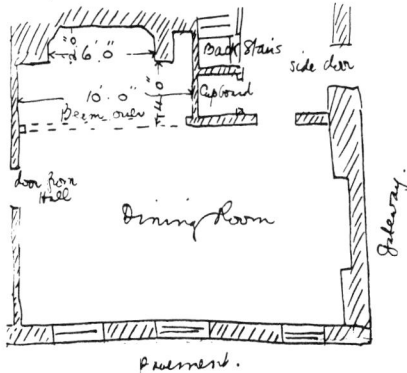

Part of a letter from R. J. Thomas, occupier of The Chantry (No. 8 Church Street) incorporating sketch plan showing location of a newly-uncovered Tudor fireplace, 1900.

hardly surprising that English Heritage raised a number of difficulties with the conversion plans and that these took time to resolve. Finally, in November 1988 the architects reported that a tender figure of £907,000, exclusive of VAT, had been negotiated for the whole project, to include landscaping and the re-roofing of the two houses. The contract with the builders, Morris Brothers (Oxford) Ltd, was signed in January 1989 and work began on the first of February 1989.

In the course of the work seven skeletons were uncovered towards the rear of the site and were duly notified to the coroner and to the County Museum. Their presence was not unexpected since much of the Church Street area was known from recent archaeological investigations to have been a medieval encroachment upon the once very extensive churchyard of the Anglo-Saxon minster church of St Mary's.

By August 1990 The Chantry was ready for occupation and the formal opening on 20 September was performed by the Venerable John Morrison, the new

Formal opening of The Chantry complex by the Venerable John Morrison, Archdeacon of Buckingham, a former Trustee, ex officio, whilst Vicar of St Mary's, on 20 September 1990. Beside him are Miss Joy Waters, Trustee since 1986, and John Leggett, Clerk to the Charity.

archdeacon of Buckingham, who as vicar of Aylesbury had until recently been the Charity's ex-officio trustee, having taken over from Canon Graham in 1982.

The completed project, with its spacious courtyard, its pleasant walkways and flower beds, fully realises the sense of "total community" aimed at by the architects. For the first-time visitor the principal sensation experienced on penetrating the low archway from Church Street and emerging from the short passage on the other side is one of surprise and delight at the unexpected vista beyond – a sensation not unlike that inspired by the courtyard gardens of old Spain. Appropriately, The Chantry is now regularly included as one of the "secret gardens of Aylesbury", large and small, which the residents open to view and for wider enjoyment.

Additional Acquisitions in Castle Street, 1990–96

While work on The Chantry project was still in progress, two other houses on the near side of Castle Street, adjacent to the new complex, had come on the market. They were No. 12 and No. 24, which were purchased in October 1990 for a total of £108,000. In November 1992 work began on a major scheme for converting these and three other cottages on the same side – Nos. 10, 14 and 22 – which had been acquired earlier, to almshouses at an estimated cost of £371,000. The conversion included the amalgamation of Nos. 22 and 24 into one dwelling, now known as No. 22 only, and was completed at the end of 1993. In June 1994 No. 16 Castle Street was purchased for £54,000 and was renovated in 1996. This was the last such purchase. When, in September 1995, the offer of development land at Green End was received it was agreed that it would not be appropriate to respond, it being observed that "there was much work to be done and money expended to bring some of the stock up to modern day standards and there was difficulty in finding occupants for some of the flats." For the present at least, the era of expansion was over.

Adjusting to Changes in Society

Completion of The Chantry brought into sharper focus the question of the existing converted accommodation on the far side of Castle Street, for it was realised that the small and awkward bed-sit flats in particular would now be even less attractive to prospective tenants. Reviewing the situation in November 1989, the trustees had concluded that "it would be logical to dispose of these properties and concentrate the Charity's properties within the triangle of the Church Street, Parsons Fee and Castle Street." In December 1992, after several tentative efforts to find a suitable purchaser had proved unsuccessful, it was reluctantly decided to reconvert Nos. 7/15 Castle Street from eight units (including five bed-sits) to five, comprising two 1-bedroom and three 2-bedroom flats and work began in 1993. Before this, in December 1991, the re-conversion of No. 12 Church Street from four units to two had been approved.

With the slackening in the pace of expansion after 1990 and the great increase in the number of almshouse places, the trustees were increasingly preoccupied with questions such as the guidelines to be applied in choosing applicants for admission to the almshouses and whether – and on what basis – to make a charge to residents, taking into account variations in individual incomes and eligibility for state benefits, etc. By December 1995 the criteria for admission had been considerably relaxed. Three years residence in Aylesbury – the minimum stated in the Scheme – was now deemed sufficient; married couples who were both of state pension age would be eligible; home owners would no longer be excluded from consideration; and savings up to £10,000 would not be a bar.

The right of the trustees to require tenants to make weekly contributions towards the maintenance of the almshouses and the services provided had been enshrined in the 1979 Scheme, but devising a simple and acceptable scale of payments proved less than straightforward and from 1990 various interim arrangements were adopted pending further consideration. Finally, in February 1995, using the audited accounts for the previous year, the cost per room per week of Council Tax, lighting and heating and other expenses was calculated and a scale of charges, ranging from £10 to £23, devised for the seven bed-sits (3 rooms), thirty-one 1-bedroom flats/houses (4 rooms) and six 2-bedroom flats/houses (5 rooms) of which the accommodation was now composed. This solution met with general acquiescence.

The issue of "pastoral care" for almspersons was raised in February 1995 following the retirement of Mr Jack Dear, an employee of James Cox and Associates, when it was realised that Mr Dear had been providing a good deal of informal support and friendship to many of the occupants in the course of performing routine maintenance chores and that his departure had left a void. In 1986 the idea of appointing a full-time warden had been considered and rejected. Now it was decided to engage as part-time pastoral care consultant Nicola Beattie, a trained nurse specialising in the care of the elderly.

Relief in Need: Hickman's and the Wider Community

Although no longer strictly required by the 1979 Scheme, the customary annual cash distribution continued to be kept up, though with some up-dating of the mode of delivery. In 1986 the practice of taking cash to the church for distribution was discontinued and cheques were substituted; soon afterwards the cheques were being sent by post. In 1986, too, it was decided that in future fresh applications would be sought by advertising and that existing recipients on the gift list would be so informed. Accordingly the following year an advertisement was placed, with the result that no fewer than 657 applications were received from septuagenarians living in Aylesbury. This figure rose steadily year by year thereafter until in 1993, by which time the amount of the gift had also risen from £15 to £20 a head, approximately 1,900 applications were received. After this, judicious rewording of the advertisement to discourage those not in real need from applying, together with a policy of allowing only one cash gift per married couple, reduced the number to more manageable proportions.

The most innovative section of the 1979 Scheme had been that headed Relief in Need, which conferred wide discretionary powers on the trustees to relieve need, hardship or distress. In the immediate aftermath of the Scheme expenditure relating to the almshouses had first call on resources, but substantial grants were also made to several local institutions, including Aylesbury Youth Action (for projects to benefit the elderly), Calibre, the Aylesbury-based cassette library for the disabled, and the Jonathan Page adventure playground. Beginning in 1980, too, a series of grants was made to the St Mary's Centre towards the salary of a community worker.

From 1990 onwards the trustees gave more sustained attention to informing themselves about Aylesbury's social problems, particularly in the area of housing provision. In 1995, for example, they commissioned a report on housing need in the town. Discussing it in January of the following year, they decided that their emphasis must remain with housing for the elderly but with the possibility of joint ventures with – or in support of – other agencies meeting a need where the trustees were unable to assume direct responsibility.

Appendix A

Trustees of Hickman's Charity from 1847

Trustees appointed by Court of Chancery

1847   Charles Hickman
          Rev. J.R. Pretyman
          Z.D. Hunt

1855	Rev. Edward Bickersteth	*in the room of*	J.R.Pretyman
1867	Rev. William Hickman	*in the room of*	C.Hickman (died)
1873	H.A.P. Cooper	*in the room of*	Z.D.Hunt
1877	Rev. A.T. Lloyd	*in the room of*	E. Bickersteth
1883	Rev. C.C. Mackarness	*in the room of*	A.T. Lloyd
1890	Rev. H.B. McNair	*in the room of*	C.C. Mackarness
1891	Thomas Horwood	*in the room of*	H.A.P. Cooper
1895	Rev. C.O. Phipps	*in the room of*	H.B. McNair
1915	Rev. V.L. Whitechurch	*in the room of*	C.O. Phipps
1922	J.W. Reader	*in the room of*	W. Hickman (died)
	James East	*in the room of*	T. Horwood
1923	Rev. C. S. Pepys	*in the room of*	V.L. Whitechurch
1925	E.S. Mackrill	*in the room of*	J. East (died)
1927	Rev. F.J. Howard	*in the room of*	C.S. Pepys
1942	A.T. Atkins	*in the room of*	J.W. Reader (died)
1944	E.P. Gilkes	*in the room of*	H.T. Atkins
1945	L.E. Button	*in the room of*	E.P. Gilkes (died)
1947	Rev. H.A. Byard	*in the room of*	F.J. Howard
1948	Reginald Davey	*in the room of*	E.S. Mackrill (died)
1955	W.H.E. Gilkes	*in the room of*	L.E. Button (died)
1964	Hayward Parrott	*in the room of*	W.H.E. Gilkes (died)
1968	L.H.E. Gilkes	*in the room of*	R. Davey
1973	Rev. Peter Graham	*in the room of*	H.A. Byard

Additional Trustees under new Charity Commission Scheme

1979   W.H. Harman
       P.F. Ryan

1981	H.G.J. Spittles	*in the room of*	P.F. Ryan
1982	E.A. Moore	*in the room of*	H. Parrott
	Rev. J.A. Morrison	*in the room of*	P. Graham
1986	Miss L.J. Walters	*in the room of*	H.G.J. Spittles
1988	J.E. Elsom	*in the room of*	L.H.E. Gilkes
1990	Rev. L.E. Pepper	*in the room of*	J.A. Morrison
	Rev. Timothy Higgins	*in the room of*	L.E. Pepper
1993	Graham Aylett	*in the room of*	J.E. Elsom
1997	Mrs Anne Atkinson	*in the room of*	W.H. Harman

Appendix B

Abstract of the will of Thomas Hickman

Preamble

States that the testator (T) is of good health and memory, revokes all previous wills by him made, commits his soul to God "trusting to be saved through the merits of Jesus Christ" and his body to be buried "in the grave of my dear mother digged as deep again as any grave is now adays made".

Devise of Landed Property

To his loving kinsmen Robert Hickman of Aylesbury, carpenter, Joseph Claydon of Bishopstone, yeoman, and John Plater the younger of Haddenham, yeoman [trustees], and to their heirs and never to be sold: his messuage in Temple Street with the backside and brick walls and appurtenances wherein T now dwells which he purchased of Thomas Dawson, gent.; 5 cottages near unto the church gate which T purchased of Joseph Payne, now in the several occupations of Thomas Harris, late of Francis Carter, Dorothy Miles and the widow Hill and Elizabeth Due, spinster; messuage or tenement in the market place which T purchased of Edward Kitson, the messuage of John Heywood on the west part and the passage to the King's Head on the east part; messuage, cottage or farm house in Walton in the parish of Aylesbury with all stalls, barns, yards, gardens, orchards and backsides and outlets thereto belonging and 21 acres of arable land, leys and meadow ground belonging to the said messuage, which T lately purchased of Thomas Deering the elder and now are in his occupation; 3½ acres of arable land in Walton fields which T purchased of Alexander Trott, now in the occupation of John Jordan; 4 acres of arable and lea ground in Walton fields now or late in the occupation of John Christmas which T purchased of him; 3½ acres of arable which T purchased of Nathaniel Birch, gent., in Walton fields, now in the occupation of Benjamin Deering and Thomas Francklin, all to be held by the trustees to the several uses, intents and purposes declared, viz.

The trustees are to let and set the said premises to the best advantage of rents, keeping them in good repair, and with the overplus of the yearly rents to raise the sum of £100 to be put out, to pay the interest thereof yearly to T's cousin Mary Day, if then living, and so long as she shall live, and after her decease to pay the said £100 to T's cousin Charles Withers, her son, but if she die before he is age 25 the interest is to be paid him till then and the said £100 to be paid him at 25, but if he die before that age then it is not to be paid but to his mother, if living, but if both die before then not to be paid at all. Immediately after the said sum of £100 is raised and paid the further sum of £100 is to be raised out of the rents and paid to T's cousin Joseph Hickman and his 3 children [not named] to be divided among them and to pay them £20 at a time as they can raise it till the said £100 be all paid. Immediately after this is paid a further sum of £100 is to be similarly raised to be paid to T's cousin William Hickman, deceased, his 3 daughters viz. Elizabeth, Sarah and Mary, to be equally divided amongst them. Immediately after this is paid a further £100 is to be similarly raised and distributed amongst the children and grandchildren representing such children that shall be then living of T's late cousin Elizabeth Nelson, deceased, eldest daughter of T's uncle Robert Hickman. Immediately after this is paid £100 more is to be similarly raised and paid to the children of T's late cousin Mary Humphrey, deceased younger daughter of the said uncle Robert, as shall be then living, to be divided amongst them.

The trustees are to have 20s. apiece yearly for their care, pain and trouble in paying the said legacies. After the legacies have been raised and paid the trustees and the churchwardens and overseers of the poor of Aylesbury are to apply all the yearly rents and profits of the premises which shall be over and above the yearly repairs of the same in alms to the poorest and most pitiful objects of charity (see extract in Chapter 1); and after the legacies paid the 5 cottages are to be almshouses for the poor people of Aylesbury, with proviso in favour of T's kin (see extract in Chapter 1).

Bequests

To T's cousin Faith Plater, who now lives with him, £30 and £20 which Mr Richard Ingoldsby and Mr Thomas Goodson owe him upon bonds and the trustees are directed to spend the £30 Mrs Trendall owes T on a surrender of her house on T's funeral expenses and the £10 Thomas Brooks owes him on bond and the £5 Mr Thomas Ligo owes him on a bill of his hand are to be given to the poorest and most pitiful objects of charity in Aylesbury.

To T's cousin Robert Hickman all his books and mathematical instruments, except any good books that T's cousin Faith may like to read.

To the poor of Wendover 30s. and of Great Brickhill 30s.

To T's cousin Grace Browne 20s. and to her children 10s. apiece.
To T's cousin Francis Claydon's children 10s apiece.
To T's cousin John Plater's children 10s. apiece.
To the children of T's deceased cousin Richard Jarvice.
To the children of T's deceased cousin Munday 10s. apiece.

The residue of T's goods and chattels, money, plate, rings and other things to T's said cousin Robert Hickman and his said cousin Faith Plater, who are made joint and sole executors.

T's loving friend, Doctor John Willson (*sic*) of Hartwell is desired to be an overseer of the will and is to have 20s. for his pains and trouble therein.

T wishes to have all things performed according to this his will written with his own hand.

Witnesses: William Hunt, John Piddington, Hester Piddington.

Codicil

Devises all the lands, etc.[not specified], as well copyhold as freehold, which T lately purchased from one Thomas Hoare to the trustees [named] named in the will in trust to sell so soon as they conveniently can so much thereof as shall pay and satisfy all T's debts and legacies and the trustees are to stand seised of the residue in trust to dispose of the rents and profits thereof to and amongst the poor of the parish of Aylesbury by such hands and in such manner and form as they are directed to dispose of T's other lands and tenements mentioned in the will to and for the use of the said poor.

Devises to T's servant Katherine Plater for term of her life the said messuage or cottage in Aylesbury wherein Thomas Harris now dwells and after her decease and not before the trustees are to dispose thereof and of the rents and profits thereof as described by the will.

19 April 1698 Thomas Hickman his mark.

Witnesses; William Busby, Francis Tyring[ham], Thomas Smith.

Probate

Certificate [Latin] that the will was proved on 24 July 1699 before Isaac Lodington, M.A., surrogate of Doctor William Foster, L.D., official of the peculiar and exempt jurisdiction of the prebendary of the prebend of Aylesbury, and that execution was granted to Robert Hickman and Faith Hitchendon *alias* Plater, now wife of Matthew Hitchendon, the executors named in the will.

BRO D/A/We/45/169

Appendix C

Thomas Dawson (d. 1677) and No. 1 Church Street

In his will Thomas Hickman states that the house in which he then dwelt had been purchased from "Thomas Dawson, gent.". This information does not necessarily imply that his predecessor had actually resided in the house, or even in Aylesbury, but numerous entries relating to births, 1653–1671 (including a son called Thomas, baptised in January 1659) and burials, 1671–1676, of the children of a Thomas Dawson, described variously as "Mr" and "gent", are found in the Aylesbury parish register, ending with his own burial in July 1677. In April 1655, too, Thomas Dawson is named in the register among those parishioners, headed by the intruded Presbyterian minister, John Luff, who nominated a replacement civil registrar under the 1653 Marriage Act (Gibbs, Aylesbury, p. 345).

In the graduated poll tax of 1660 (BRO D/LE/17/3) Thomas Dawson was assessed at 3s, on his property, while his wife, Mary, paid the usual flat rate of 6d. No other Dawsons are taxed, although several baptisms of children of a John Dawson are also listed in the parish register between 1650 and 1655 (including another Thomas, baptised in 1653). In 1661–2, in the immediate aftermath of the Restoration, Thomas Dawson, described as "gentleman" (*generosus*) served as churchwarden and, as late as August 1662, was still being pursued, together with his two co-wardens, for failing to produce a bill of presentments to the newly reconstituted Church of England authorities. His excuse for non-appearance on one occasion was that he had gone to London with a prisoner (E. R. C. Brinkworth (ed.), *Episcopal Visitation Book for the Archdeaconry of Buckingham, 1662*, Bucks Record Soc. 1947, pp. 29–30).

In the light of this information it seems safe to identify Thomas Dawson with the undersheriff of that name who signed an official letter on behalf of the sheriff, dated at Aylesbury, in 1651 (G. Eland, *Papers from an Iron Chest*, 1937, p. 82) and who is mentioned ("Mr Dawson … the undersheriff") the same year in a letter filed among the Archdeaconry probate records (BRO D/A/Wf/38/97); and also with the Thomas Dawson who was clerk of the peace for Buckinghamshire from 1653 to 1658, and possibly longer (his predecessor's only known date is 1647 and his successor was in office by 1664), but of whom nothing more is known (Stephens, *The Clerks of the Counties*, p. 58). The undersheriff was, and is, responsible for the routine duties of the sheriff; the clerk of the peace was the principal officer of the court of Quarter Sessions. Both offices required someone with legal expertise.

An undated draft manorial survey of the 1650s shows Thomas Dawson, gentleman, owning a tenement and garden in Baker Row, for which he owed suit of court only (BRO D/X 1007/22). His name appears in the two property tax assessments of 1668 and 1673 for which assessments have been preserved, both of which are arranged in alphabetical order of surnames. In the earlier of these Thomas Dawson, gent, is assessed to pay 5s. (no other details are given), but in 1673 there are two consecutive entries, both of which, unusually, are placed out of alphabetical order among the names beginning with "H". They read as follows:

Mr Dawsons (*sic*) for his house	00 02 01
More for Mr Gurnyes	00 02 08

In the first entry the words "for his" are interlineated and several words have been cancelled at the beginning of the line. On closer inspection it can be seen that the original reading was:

Tho. Hickman for Mr Dawsons house

In context the alteration is clearly significant for the association between the two names can hardly be accidental. The most likely explanation would seem to be that the mistake arose because Thomas Hickman (who is presumably the founder and not his father) was the actual occupant the house, or part of it, at this time but was not the legal occupier for tax purposes. Liability for payment of the tax fell on occupiers rather than owners if the two were not the same, (so that, for example, Sir John Pakington's name does not appear in the assessment because all his demesne properties were let to tenants), but the actual occupant, who might be a sub-tenant or lodger, would not necessarily be named in the assessment.

It is possible that Thomas Hickman, in line with his later financial transactions, had also advanced money on mortgage and was able to acquire the house on Dawson's death in 1677. The fate of the Dawson family after this date is obscure. There is, indeed, a solitary reference in 1679 to a Thomas Dawson among Aylesbury property owners who were fined by the court of Quarter Sessions for defaulting on their obligation to maintain the parish highways (*Bucks Sessions Records*, vol. 1, p. 27), but this could well be an out-of-date reference to the deceased Thomas, since it appears that the original presentment of the offence must date back to before 1678, when the existing sessions records begin. During the following quarter century the parish register records only the births of daughters of John Dowson (*sic*) in 1692 and 1694 and the burial in 1703 of Mary Dawson, widow.

Appendix D

Notes on the Previous Owners and Occupiers of Charity Properties Acquired Since 1970

These notes are based principally on the title deeds of the properties concerned, few of which date back earlier than 1850 though in some cases the names (but no dates or other details) of several successive earlier occupiers are recited. Limited use has also been made of the parish register, contemporary directories (from 1792), published census transcripts for 1851 and 1891 and of Rutt's *Eye-Draught* (1809; see p. 51). These sources are indicated by a date in round brackets; it should be borne in mind that there are no street numbers before 1891 so that identification is not always straightforward. See also location plan on pp. 118–19.

Church Street

No. 4

This small, plain building was formerly part of a block of property comprising Nos. 2, 4, and 6 Church Street and 14 Temple Square which formed part of the ancient endowment of John Bedford's Charity, founded in 1494, and which had always been let to tenants. It may have been built, or rebuilt, around the same time as the adjoining house, No. 2 Church Street, which has the date 1809 incised in one of the bricks. The right-hand side of the building was originally a one-storey extension; the upper floor on that side was added in the 1980s. In 1921, with the consent of the Charity Commissioners, the whole block had been sold to Messrs G. M. Brown of Tring, estate agents. No. 4 was sold the following year to F. H. Samuels, employment exchange manager, from whom it was repurchased in 1948. The vendors in 1978 were trustees for W. Brown & Co. (Investments), in liquidation. An upper room belonging to the owner of the adjoining house (No. 2) had to be acquired separately.

No. 8 (The Chantry)

The earliest deed abstract shows that the house was in the ownership and occupation of Robert Gibbs (1816–1893), auctioneer, the historian, by 1859. Names of previous occupiers recited are Francis Mangie (gentleman, d. 1750), Joseph Grimes and John Plomer. Mangie is styled "captain" in 1720 in an index to Sun Fire insurance records (BRO); Grimes seems to have been a laceman (1792). After this, the house is stated to have been divided into two dwellings in the several occupations of Mary Plomer, widow, William Young, the Reverend John Rawbone (1809) and John Harris (1809). Rawbone was master of the grammar school from

Sketch of Nos 8 and 10 Church Street by H. J. Cox of JCA, architects to the Charity. During restoration most of the gable bargeboards and finials on No. 8 were found to be decayed and were replaced by exact replicas.

1806 to 1813. Harris was Aylesbury's last, and much respected Presbyterian minister; he died in retirement in London in 1829 aged 76.

Subsequently the house was again made into one dwelling occupied in succession by Charles Mitchell Terry (1830, 1842, 1847), Henry Beresford Pickess (1853), both surgeons, and Thomas Thorpe. Terry, born 1791 at Waddesdon, was a member of the well-known Aylesbury firm of brewers, but little else is known about him. The land tax returns in the County Record Office seem to confirm that he was owner of both parts of the then divided property by 1825 and was himself occupying one of them until around 1832, when he was occupying both. It thus looks as if the credit for the present delightful gothic facade, dated on stylistic grounds to *c.* 1830–1840, belongs to him.

The 1891 census shows Robert Gibbs, "author and printer", sharing No. 8 with his two spinster daughters, Mary and Elizabeth (Eliza) and a single maidservant. After Gibbs's death in 1893 his daughters moved away from Aylesbury. By 1900 they were living in Broadstairs and the house, then known as Oak Hall, was let to Mr R. J. Thomas, who later purchased the freehold in 1913. As county surveyor from 1890 until his death, aged 58, in 1921 Thomas was responsible for Buckinghamshire's roads during the early days of the motor car. A native of Carnarvon, he was a personal friend of David Lloyd George (prime minister, 1919–22), whose wife called frequently to enquire after him during his last illness.

In 1922 the house was sold to A. W. D. Coventon, an Aylesbury G.P., who erected a separate surgery at the rear on the right-hand side of the carriage entrance passage, following an exchange of land with the owner of No. 10. In 1946 the property was acquired by the medical partnership of Hancock, Good and Gimson. In 1961 one of the partners, Dr Peter Allen Gimson, who had previously leased the property, purchased the freehold. Dr Gimson spent many years researching the history of turnpike roads in Bucks and his papers are now in the County Record Office. He and his wife continued to live at The Chantry until 1975, when they sold to Piers and Cheryl Morgan.

No. 10

According to the earliest deed of 1862 it was "formerly called the Plough". The Plough is one of several properties listed in a grant of Crown properties in 1553 cited by Robert Gibbs in *Local Occurrences* (1878), which in context probably means that it had belonged to a religious foundation of some kind before the Reformation (e.g. a chantry to endow the celebration of masses for the dead). The Plough is mentioned again in the will of John Keble (see p. 23), proved in 1601, but no later references to it have been found. Gibbs asserts (*Aylesbury*, pp. 427–8) that the house was for a time the residence of a branch of the ancient landed family of Croke, of Chilton, Bucks, and Studley in Oxfordshire. William Croke and his nephew Alexander (1728–77) were both stewards of manors in Aylesbury – and thus by definition lawyers – the former in 1737–42 and the latter in 1766. Parish register entries, correspondence and other miscellaneous papers in the County Record Office confirm that there was a continuous family presence in the town between the 1720s and the 1760s. Alexander Croke was resident from around 1754, when he married the daughter of a local vicar, and his son, the future Sir Alexander Croke (1758–1842), an eminent lawyer (*Dictionary of National Biography*) was baptised in the parish church. Gibbs says that Sir Alexander was believed locally to have been born in a house in Back (Buckingham) Street, but Church Street seems a more likely address. Alexander, senior, seems to have retained a connection with Aylesbury even after he inherited the Studley Priory estate in 1766, but the link ceased with his death in 1777.

The 1862 deed is a conveyance to Thomas Horwood, gentleman, from William Young Pursell and other members of the Horwood and Pursell families. The occupier in 1862 was Ann Harman. Previous occupiers are listed as Daniel Lathwell ("esquire", 1792; 1809), Patty Bartlett, widow (1842), and David Lymington, while the 1851 census seems to show Robert Judd, stationmaster, as the occupier at that date. Mrs Bartlett was by birth a Russell and family correspondence in the County Record Office (D/X 685/2) confirms that she was living in Broad (i.e. Church) Street by 1836, where she kept a day and boarding school for young ladies.

Major (later Colonel) Horwood, the owner in 1862, was a partner in the firm of Horwood and James, solicitors, then of Temple Square. By 1874 he was himself occupying No. 10 and he seems to have had a tenancy of No. 12 also. In 1891, the year he became a trustee of Thomas Hickman's Charity, the census shows him, aged 62, living at No. 12 (No. 10 is not separately listed) with his wife, their seven children (six of them female) and resident governess, cook, nurse, housemaid and coachman. By 1900 Horwood had moved away and No. 10 was occupied by his tenant, Mr G. T. Hunt. In 1919 Hunt purchased the freehold and also that of the two adjoining houses, Nos. 12 and 14, which Horwood had acquired in 1905. In 1931 Hunt sold No. 10 to Major Coningsby Ralph Disraeli (1867–1936) of Hughenden Manor, a county councillor and the nephew and heir of Benjamin Disraeli, the prime minister. Major Disraeli re-sold in 1934 to David Provan, an engineer, from whom it was purchased in 1939 by the Equitable Life Assurance Society, the vendors in 1985. During the 1970s the property was leased as office accommodation by Saccone and Speed and Courage Ltd.

After it was acquired by the Charity urgently needed structural repairs to No. 10 revealed that at the time the present Georgian facade was added the roof of the medieval frame had been raised by some two metres in order to create additional space, allowing the insertion of the three large dormer windows which are a feature of the house. The large three-storey extension at the rear of the house appears to be a later addition.

Note. Both No. 8 and No. 10 are Grade II Star listed buildings.

No. 12 (formerly No. 12 and No. 14)

The deeds begin with a conveyance of both houses from the trustees of the will of Henry White of Hampstead, retired surveyor, to James Battin of Thame, gentleman,

Sketch by H. J. Cox of No. 12 Church Street as restored in 1978.

in 1845. The respective occupiers at that date were [Miss Sarah] Hilliard (1842, 1851) and [John] Bunce; previous occupiers being named as Miss Neale (1809) and Mrs Ivatts (1809). It was also stated that the house occupied by Hilliard [No. 14] had formerly been two dwellings. Miss Neale and Miss Hilliard were doubtless related to Robert Neale (d. 1777) and his nephew, John Hilliard (d. 1814), who had held the post of writing master at the grammar school in succession.

There are no more deeds until 1905, when Thomas Horwood purchased both properties, the unlikely vendor being H. J. Stacey, a hospital attendant living at Little Bay, near Sydney, New South Wales. The occupiers were Albert Bailey (No. 12) and Henry King, previously Thomas Horwood and George Nicholls. The latter, a printer-compositor, had been resident in 1891, aged 56, with his wife, 53, son, 14, and a sixteen-year-old female servant. In 1919, when Horwood sold both houses to G. T. Hunt, the occupiers were Albert Bailey and Mrs A. May.

In 1921 No. 14 was purchased by Miriam Barstow, who sold it in 1930 to Miss Octavia Liberty of The Prebendal, Aylesbury. Miss Liberty was a sister of Sir Arthur Lasenby Liberty (1843–1917), founder of Liberty's, the famous London store. In the following year she also acquired No. 12 from Hunt and converted the two houses into one, thenceforth, known as No. 12. Following Miss Liberty's death the house was sold in 1950 to Mr Elliott Viney, then of Green End House. Later purchasers were: R. S. Wallace, a London architect, in 1953; Dr Lorenz Michaelis, a specialist at Stoke Mandeville Hospital, and his wife Gabrielle, both refugees from Hitler's Germany, in 1961; and Mrs Ada Ritchie (d. 1973) in 1964.

Castle Street

The houses in upper Castle Street are smaller and individually much less important as buildings than those in Church Street, though all are statutorily listed either in their own right or for their group value. The street's situation on what by 1750 had become a busy through-route to Oxford probably made it unattractive to wealthier residents.

South Side

Nos. 7, 9 and 11

These three cottages were originally one house, built in the late seventeenth or early eighteenth century, but had been subdivided before 1809 by the insertion of flimsy wattle and daub partition walls which left floor areas at different levels of

Almshouses on the south side of Castle Street (Nos 11–17).

the same house out of alignment. By 1881, when the deeds begin, all three were in the ownership of Elizabeth, widow of John Darvill, a baker, who had inherited the property from her father, William Baldwin, shoemaker (d. 1851). By 1885 the three houses had been bought by the Vale of Aylesbury Oddfellows Friendly Society, who sold them in 1895 to G. T. Weston (d. 1934), a hairdresser, whose daughter sold to Castle Properties Ltd in 1951. During all this period, and earlier, the cottages had been let to a variety of tenants. In 1891 the occupants were: (No. 7) Selina Hitchcock, staymaker, aged 58, and Jane Bunce, lodger, 58; (No. 9) James Tate, county court bailiff, aged 37, his wife, 34, and daughter, 14, and (No. 11) Francis Slade, billposter, aged 24, his wife, two children, grandfather, Joseph Tayler, 81, described as "town cryer", and female servant, 13.

No. 13

This was originally one dwelling with No. 15 and is of seventeenth-century date. By the mid eighteenth century No. 13 had itself been subdivided and was occupied as two dwellings until around 1804. The owners from 1777 were successively

Thomas Eggleton, shopkeeper otherwise haberdasher; William Lawrence, bricklayer; George Hanwell, fruiterer, 1784; Richard Willgoss, tailor (later described as
a gentleman), 1789; and William Clark, tailor, 1804. William Clark (1809) lived in
the house from 1804 until his death in 1831. In 1832 unpaid mortgage debts
forced his daughter, Sarah Clark, to relinquish the property and it was sold to John
Barnaby, a corn dealer, who died the same year. His son George (b. *c.* 1835), a
groom at Crafton in the parish of Mentmore, lived in the house with his wife from
1881 until 1913, when he gave it to his unmarried daughter Harriet, who had
stayed at home to look after her parents. In 1921 Harriet sold to George Clarke,
(d. 1930) a caretaker, whose widow sold to Frederick Adams, a builder, in 1936.
Castle Properties Ltd purchased it from Mrs D. O. Weedon, a widow, in 1961.

No. 15

Richard Willgoss, tailor, bought this house in 1788 from William Baker, a builder,
of Berkhamsted, who had recently converted an adjacent house for use as a
Nonconformist chapel of which he himself became the first minister. The
purchase deed included the right to connect pipes to the well under, or near, the
chapel. Willgoss was the occupier in 1809, but sold it in 1812 to William Bunce,
basketmaker, otherwise cordwainer (i.e. shoemaker). After Bunce's death in 1814
the property descended jointly to his two daughters, one of whom, Jane, married
Thomas White, carpenter. Jane, aged 47, described as a seamstress, and Thomas,
48, were living there in 1851 with their two children, aged 7 and 10, and lodger,
Anna Clarke, 84. White was still the occupier in 1859, when he sold his interest to
William Woollhead of Thornborough, near Buckingham, to whom he owed
money on mortgage. In 1868 the house passed by purchase to William Nicholls,
corn dealer, who was living there in retirement, aged 69 in 1891 with his two
nieces, Alice Matthews aged 12, and Anne J. Hawkins, spinster, 31, housekeeper.
On his death in 1900 Nicholls left the property to his wife's niece, Jane Hawkins,
who sold it in 1920 to the tenant, Stanislaus Soutien Longley (1894–*c.* 1967), an
artist who specialised in watercolour landscape and decorative figure painting. In
1958 Longley, then resident in Brighton, sold to W. H. E. Gilkes, who sold to
Castle Properties Ltd the following year.

No. 17 (site of chapel)

Information on the chapel and the successive congregations who worshipped
there is to be found in Robert Gibbs's *History of Aylesbury* (1885), pp. 445–47. All
that now survives is the minister's house next door (No. 19) and the remains of

the old burial ground, now a private garden, behind it, where many members of the Gibbs family and their relations the Rolls and the Paynes were interred. Recitals in the deeds indicate that the freehold of the premises was conveyed by Richard Willgoss in 1803 to Arthur Charles Stone, John Rolls, James Neale, Samuel Goode, Benjamin Loader and William Sanders, as trustees of what was later known as the Protestant Dissenting Chapel and Minister's House Charity. In 1937, after the chapel, then known as the Castle Street Hall, had long ceased to be used for worship, the trustees sold it, with the cottage (No. 19) and garden, to Unity Halls (Aylesbury) Ltd. In 1978, Unity Halls Ltd being in liquidation, the hall was sold to the trustees of Aylesbury Constituency Labour Party, who were the vendors in 1980.

North Side

The houses on this side all form part of a continuous range (Nos. 10–24) of eighteenth-century cottages fronting a raised terrace created by a lowering of the street

Hickman's most recently converted houses, 10–16 and 22 on the north side of Castle St., which share their gardens with the Chantry.

level probably executed in the 1750s in order to reduce the gradients of the hill for the benefit of wheeled traffic. Projecting ground-floor period windows on Nos. 22 and 24 suggest earlier use as shops and the dimensions of window arches on some of the other houses are also indicative of the windows having been larger.

Nos. 10 and 12

These two houses were originally one and, until the lowering of the street level made it redundant, the ground floor of No. 10 was a carriage entrance, the faint outline of which can still be seen in the rendering. As a result of the subdivision, part of No. 10 was situated to the rear of No. 12. The deeds show that by the early nineteenth century both houses formed part of the estate of James James (d. 1846), solicitor. In 1871 they were purchased by Thomas Horwood, a partner in the same firm. In 1899 he sold them to Mary Ludgate, wife of Daniel, a bootmaker, who was living at No. 10 when she died in 1914, after which both houses were sold to Rose Pieroni, a widow. On Mrs Pieroni's death in 1921 No. 10 was sold to Eliza Maria Haynes; on her death in 1955 it was acquired by the then occupier, Mrs Lydia Read (d. 1971), whose personal representatives were the vendors in 1984.

No. 12 had been sold in 1921 to the occupier, Mr Thomas Brown, a fishmonger, whose son Frederick inherited in 1946 and was living there when he died in 1989. As late as the 1930s fish was being sold from a room in the house and even after the war Fred Brown and his wife Gladys operated a fish round of local villages as far afield as Kimble and Princes Risborough.

The occupiers in 1891 were: (No. 10) Frederick Barlow, shoemaker, aged 63, and his wife Harriet, 48; and (No. 12) Frederick Brown, fishmonger, aged 26, his wife Minnie, 24, and their four infant children.

Nos. 14 and 16

From recitals in the earliest deed, dated 1828, we learn that these two cottages, with a third cottage adjoining, were erected in, or shortly before, the year 1780 on the site of a house and premises purchased from Sir Herbert Perrott Pakington, baronet, lord of the manor of Aylesbury. The entrepreneur responsible for this early exercise in redevelopment was James Lee (d. 1780), "innholder", who kept the Angel inn in Kingsbury and was related by marriage to the Read family, brickmakers, of Aylesbury. The previous occupier of the site had been none other than **William Hickman** (1716–77), carpenter, founder of the junior branch of the Aylesbury Hickmans (see p. 25). Here then was where the family carpentry business had been carried on for over a century.

The 1828 deed is a conveyance of both cottages, each said to comprise a dwelling room, bedroom and attic and then in the occupation of Juffs and Barnes, from Lee's heirs, John and Richard Read, to Richard Atkins, cordwainer, who was living in one of them when he died in 1850. In his will Mr Atkins lists some of his personal possessions in unusual detail. To his brother, John Atkins of Buckingham, also a shoemaker, he gave "my three best suits of Clothes, namely my coloured Suit equal to new, my Suit of black clothes, and my suit consisting of my blue Coat, drab Trowsers and buff Waistcoat, with an extra Waistcoat", together with "my Clothes Box to put the said three Suits of Clothes in". His sister, Elizabeth Juffs received "my Watch, gold Seal and Key and also my Snuff Box and gold Broach." Clearly Mr Atkins was able to cut a highly respectable figure.

Under Richard Atkins's will the cottages descended to his nephew, William Atkins, a tailor, who was occupying one of them in 1863, when he sold to Thomas Wootton of Aylesbury, innkeeper. From Wootton the cottages passed by sale in 1877 to George Marks, a baker, whose son William, a grocer at Tring, inherited in 1906 and sold them in 1919 to Robert Nappin, a corn merchant, then living at No. 41 Castle Street. Nappin sold No. 16 to Frederick Adams, a builder, in 1936, but was living at No. 14 when he died in 1946, when it was sold to Florence Coulson, widow (d. 1948). Mrs Coulson's heir, Ann Dixon, was resident in 1964, when she sold to Mrs Janie Wilson (d. 1983). Mrs Wilson's personal representatives were the vendors in 1983.

Meanwhile No. 16 had passed in succession to W. J. Burnham, retired dairy inspector, in 1936, then to R. D. and H. R. Murdoch in 1953 and finally, in 1972, to N. L. Adams of Weedon, an engineer, and his wife.

The occupants in 1891 were: (No. 14) John Fellows, aged 58, a bricklayer, his unmarried daughter and housekeeper Elizabeth, 25, son William, 18, a plumber, and Thomas, 15, a telegraph messenger, and two younger sons, aged 10 and 13; and (No. 16) James Miller, aged 58, a county court bailiff, his wife Sarah, 60 and lodger, Samuel Winn, 15, a printer's labourer.

No. 22

The deeds take us back only to 1948, when Eliza Haynes (see note on Nos. 10 and 12) appears to have been left the property under the will of Eliza Brown, widow. In 1957 it was purchased by Mrs A. M. Brown, who sold to Annie and Alexander Beckett of Whitchurch in 1978. The vendors in 1986 were C. and G. Kubale.

The occupants in 1891 were James Prunty, aged 60, bird cage maker, and his sister Mary Prunty, 68, a retired dressmaker.

No. 24

Frances Putnam, spinster, of Aylesbury inherited this property under the will of her aunt, Mrs Ann Bennion (d. 1857), who had been living there, aged 60, in 1851. In 1861 she conveyed it to her niece, Mary Jane Putnam (d. 1884), who left it to trustees for her young niece, Elizabeth Holden (afterwards Clansey) of Liverpool. In 1900 it was sold to Richard Callon (d. 1912) of Aylesbury, an engineer following whose death it was sold to Mr E. C. Tofield, a printer, in 1914. Successive deeds between 1899 and 1914 give the occupier as Harry Turner. In 1929 Mr Tofield sold to Mrs Ethel Stanford, wife of Jack Stanford, a labourer. In 1937 Mrs Stanford sold to William Oldham, scrap metal dealer, who sold in 1944 to George Comerford of Bierton, draper, who re-sold in 1949 to Charles Poulton of High Street, Aylesbury, a blacksmith, originally from Tring, who was living at No. 24 when he died in 1970. His widow survived until 1990, when the house was sold to the Charity.

The sole occupier in 1891 was James Ivines, aged 67, an agricultural labourer.

Location plan of the almshouses.

Church

ST MARY'S SQUARE

Parish
Hall

PEBBLE LANE

PH

PH

Museum

Victoria
Club

CHURCH STREET

to 11

1 to 5

4 & 4a

Walker
House

Castle Close

GEORGE STREET

LB

PH

TEMPLE
SQUARE

TEMPLE S